Resisting Discrimination

Affirmative Strategies for Principals and Teachers

Louis F. Mirón

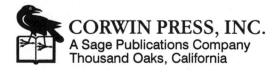
CORWIN PRESS, INC.
A Sage Publications Company
Thousand Oaks, California

136702

For information address:

Corwin Press, Inc.
A Sage Publications Company
2455 Teller Road
Thousand Oaks, California 91320
e-mail: order@corwin.sagepub.com

SAGE Publications Ltd.
6 Bonhill Street
London EC2A 4PU
United Kingdom

SAGE Publications India Pvt. Ltd.
M-32 Market
Greater Kailash I
New Delhi 110 048 India

Printed in the United States of America

Library of Congress Cataloging-in-Publication Data

Mirón, Louis F.
    Resisting discrimination : affirmative strategies for principals and teachers / Louis F. Mirón.
        p.   cm.
    Includes bibliographical references and index.
    ISBN 0-8039-6422-6 (cloth : alk. paper). — ISBN 0-8039-6423-4 (pbk. : alk. paper)
    1. Discrimination in education—United States—Prevention.
I. Title.
LC212.62.M57   1996
370.19'342—dc20   96-28059

This book is printed on acid-free paper.

97 98 99 00 01 10 9 8 7 6 5 4 3 2 1

Corwin Press Production Editor: S. Marlene Head
Editorial Assistant: Nicole Fountain
Typesetter: Rebecca Evans
Cover Designer: Marcia R. Finlayson

Contents

Preface

This book presents affirmative strategies to rid schools of discrimination. I suggest practices ranging from conventional administrative leadership action to somewhat controversial "political" (local government) alliances that can improve students' everyday welfare. I conclude with a modest proposal to foster "moral development" in public education by responding progressively to classroom teachers' hierarchy of needs (such as personal safety). I also ask teachers—all of us—to embrace an "ethics of the heart" that will have the effect of upholding the spirit of racial-ethnic equality in our public schools.

Put this way, the premise of this book appears deceptively straightforward. But the truth is that for large numbers of students, public schooling is anything but straightforward. Despite promises of equal educational opportunity, minority students from lower socioeconomic groups must overcome enormous systemic educational inequalities. The disparities are usually ones of access and expectations, ranging from the concrete to the subliminal: from lack of access to high-tech equipment to ineligibility for gifted-and-talented programs. Inequality of educational outcomes is the result of a hidden curriculum that too often expects more only from students who are better prepared for schooling in the first place.

Following the letter of the law (that is, strictly adhering to state and school board policies) paradoxically undermines the law's broad aim to give all students the opportunities to succeed. My aim

viii

in writing this book is to help us motivate ourselves, as professional educators, to change our practices. In other words, principals and teachers in public schools need to pay equal attention to *practice* as well as *formal school policies*. We must honor the spirit of the law of equality and equity for racial-ethnic minority students.

Directly or indirectly through a better educated citizenry, all of us in public education have benefited from policies such as affirmative action and civil rights. However, institutional patterns change slowly.[1] Many of our students have prospered from caring, nurturing teachers and principals. But we must do much more. I hope to arouse a deeper compassion and personal conviction from educators who have not, purportedly, been beneficiaries of policies such as affirmative action. As Michael Apple has repeatedly cautioned, we can't give up on the idea of public education *simply because low-income students of color demand changes in the organization of schools*. Diversity is a value we all should embrace, not reject, in the classroom.

As researchers and educators in public schools, we have been in denial far too long about the failures of the American system to live up to its constitutional promises of equality of educational access and outcomes. One disheartening result of this denial is an all-too-common belief among minority students I have interviewed in high schools across the country that there is no racial-ethnic prejudice in their schools. They often believe that their principals and teachers treat them "no differently" from anyone else. Yet, when it comes to the level of academic expectations held by school personnel, high school students (and increasingly elementary students), both majority and minority, describe in great detail the effects of what I have come to call *academic discrimination.* Moreover, as I establish throughout the book, this type of discrimination is related to how students represent themselves in the classroom: their collective styles of dress, their ways of speaking, the colors of their skin . . . related, in other words, to their personal and collective identities.

The dream of resisting discrimination is quite ambitious. The goal of erasing the legacy of educational inequalities for large groups of students might be impossible if we continue to act alone. The message in this book is that we (the education professionals) are not the enemy of social justice for our students. Armed with a new mindfulness of the unintentional harm we sometimes inflict on our students, we can finally act on our values of participatory democracy, compassion, and fairness. We all can be educational leaders in this effort. We must, therefore, not march alone in this struggle to honor the spirit of equity and equality. Together with other leaders—our students, their families, residents in neighborhoods—we can mobilize coalitions and powerfully respond to those moral conservatives who choose to ignore the preferences already bestowed upon more advantaged students and families.

This book is about confronting the social (as distinct from the legal) reality of discrimination in our schools and taking affirmative, deliberative action to expel it from our professional legacy. The good news is that if we can eliminate the remains of institutional racism from our public schools, then we can eliminate this unconscious habit from *any* public institution. Yes, the power is in our hands! We can be free of the menace of discrimination.

LOUIS F. MIRÓN
Irvine, California
September, 1996

Note

1. As an immigrant from Guatemala in 1953, I vividly recall the ugliness of racism in the deep South as blacks mobilized for civil rights. More than 40 years later, as a professor in the University of California (UC) system, I am saddened by the Board of Regents' decision in 1996 to end affirmative action—one of the few tools available to low-income minority students to gain access to a world-class education—on UC campuses.

Acknowledgments

This book would not have been possible without the help of many practitioners who graciously read various drafts of the manuscript. In particular, Steve Keller, a school administrator and doctoral student, made numerous substantive suggestions, kept detailed notes on references, and pulled the final manuscript together. Dennis Evans provided valuable feedback by making draft chapters available to his students enrolled in courses in educational leadership at the University of California, Irvine.

My colleague, Kathy Nakagawa, provided invaluable help with her conceptualization of the "empowering" and "enabling" roles of parents in school policy that I draw upon in Chapter 7. Similarly, in Chapters 5 and 6, I abundantly cite the research my students in the Crosscultural Language and Academic Development (CLAD) and the Bilingual Crosscultural Language and Academic Development (BCLAD) summer institutes conducted to document teacher leadership strategies. Also, Cheryl Craft made sure that my editors at Corwin Press received my material in the form they needed, and in a timely fashion.

Finally, I owe a great debt to Gracia Alkema not only for the confidence she expressed in me as a writer, but also for the skillful manner in which she led me to consider a book for those on the front lines of education, the practitioners.

About the Author

Louis Mirón serves as Chair of the Department of Education at the University of California—Irvine and as Director of the Center for Collaborative Research in Education, which facilitates research projects, conferences, and publications aimed at improving K-12 schooling nationally and worldwide. Mirón holds a Ph.D. in the politics and policy of education from Tulane University, an MA in secondary education from Louisiana State University; a Graduate Teaching Certificate from UCLA; and a BA in English literature from Tulane University. He is the author of *The Social Construction of Urban Schooling* (Hampton Press, 1996).

Throughout his 10 years in academia, his personal and research interests have centered on education reform from a cultural, political, and structural perspective. While on the faculty at the University of New Orleans and Loyola University—New Orleans, Mirón was a frequent commentator in both the print and broadcast media on educational issues of local and national interest. His work resulted in legislative reforms in K–12 education, including a state constitutional change making the office of the State Superintendent of Education an appointed rather than an elected position. He served on the New Orleans Mayor's Charter Advisory Committee that redrafted the voter-approved home rule charter. As a result, the mayor and the superintendent of New Orleans schools joined forces to win approval of a $1 billion school bond issue for infrastructure improvements.

Mirón directed the first accelerated schools reform project in New Orleans, funded by Chevron Corporation.

To my parents, grandmother, and brothers
who struggled throughout their lives
to overcome racism and discrimination.

Discrimination—
Subtle and Not-So-Subtle

Public schools, like most institutions funded with taxpayer monies, must honor the laws of the country. Since the passage of the Civil Rights Act in 1964, discrimination because of race, religion, gender, or place of national origin has been forbidden. For example, it is against the law for any public school to deny admission to immigrants (legal or illegal).[1] The problem with this line of reasoning is that many principals and teachers think that if they follow the guidelines of the law, their schools will be protected from discrimination, prejudice, and racism. They may assume that following the letter of the law is inherent in honoring the spirit of the law. It is not.

Between 1993 and 1995, I conducted a study of four public high schools enrolling large percentages of ethnic and language minority students in the Deep South. The study consisted of 48 interviews lasting between 30 minutes and 90 minutes (Lauria, Mirón & Dashner, 1994; Mirón, 1996; Mirón & Lauria, 1995). We wanted to discover the extent to which students from similar socioeconomic backgrounds but varying school cultures (magnet vs. neighborhood) and with different levels of academic success (A, B grades vs. C, D grades), expressed "resistance" to both the formal and the hidden curriculum (Apple, 1985). My findings suggest that there is wide student resistance in public schooling in an urban context. This resistance, moreover, is directly tied to students' perceptions of lack of fairness and teacher stereotyping of minority students. For example,

1

students often complained that teachers believed that *all* Asian American students were "bright" and motivated, whereas African American and Latino students were not. Similarly, African American students from neighborhood schools complained that principals shut down assemblies and cultural activities because teachers were afraid for their safety. By contrast, African American students of similar socioeconomic status attending magnet schools boasted of the caring atmosphere and the rich curriculum and extracurricular activities, including numerous student assemblies. I call this phenomenon academic discrimination. The following excerpt from the study illustrates this kind of discrimination, which we widely observed in similar school settings throughout the Deep South.[2]

> A.B.: [Neighborhood High] is not all that good to me because, in the past 3 years it's changed. I like it, but it's just some of the things that go on at this school that I don't understand. Teachers' attitudes and stuff. For instance, I can sit up here and I can ask you [a teacher], 'Well, how do you do this certain problem?' And the teacher, the teacher says, 'Well, I just went over that, went over that with you. And I'm saying, 'Well, you know, I don't understand so that's why I am asking you.' [The teacher answers] 'You all are acting like you're dumb.' They wouldn't say it out loud in general, but I know they really mean it towards me. (Lauria, Mirón, & Dashner, 1994, p. 17)

Our data did not suggest that teachers and administrators deliberately set out to treat students differently in the classroom. Rather, the school culture informally, but systematically, set higher expectations for many of the white students and for the majority of Asian American students. According to several of the students we interviewed at Neighborhood High, these different expectations in and of themselves affected different achievement levels. Listen to the words of N.B.:

> Yeah, they [teachers] expect more from the Vietnamese kids, who they think are always smarter. They don't really expect us to do better. I mean, it's like the Vietnamese is always smarter, and they never expect a black student to be smarter than a Vietnamese student, you know. They automatically think that we're dumb. (Lauria, Mirón, & Dashner, 1994, p. 25)

For the most part, we did not supplement the student interviews with direct classroom observations. However, one of my doctoral students did follow up on observations and informal conversations with teachers in a junior high school. His research bore out the findings of our study of student resistance (Anfara, 1995). Whether intentional or not, teachers' expectations of academic work, as reported by students, revealed discriminatory attitudes and behavior.

The important point, I found, is that there are direct relationships among discriminatory practices, the hidden curriculum, and students' sense of self. The best of outcomes is illustrated by a student from Neighborhood High who declared she had completed her required units to graduate. She reacted assertively to accusations that she had failed to turn in assignments and to threats from a teacher who said, "I'm going to fail you." The worst possibility is that low academic expectations for poor minority youth lead to their imprisonment or dropping out of school and, as one student from City High described it, to becoming a "nameless statistic." Furthermore, these academic "failures" take the brunt of violent crime, as we have seen, adding to the public health epidemic plaguing our country (Allen, 1995, p. 13).

Academic Discrimination

Academic discrimination occurs when teachers explicitly display marked differences in expectations for the levels of academic achievement they hold for students. These varying levels of expectation are frequently tied to particular minority groups with lower income levels who come from poor neighborhoods. For example, our study found that African American students who lived in public housing, and who attended racially diverse neighborhood schools, suffered the brunt of discriminatory practices. We noted that teachers from these neighborhood schools repeatedly challenged low-income black students who scored well on tests or who claimed to have turned in "seat assignments." On the other hand, the level of trust bestowed upon Vietnamese students in the same schools seemed inordinately higher than that afforded the majority of African American students.

I do not want to be too harsh on classroom teachers. The more complex point from my study is that discrimination varies widely, depending on the "culture" of the school (Sarason, 1982). For example, one inner-city magnet school I studied had a 100% enrollment of African American students. More than 66% of these students received free or reduced-cost lunches. Many of these students also lived in poor neighborhoods or public housing developments. In other words, they represented social class backgrounds similar to those of the students from the mixed-neighborhood school. Yet in the all-black, African American school, the students unanimously praised the high academic standards and rich cultural activities. Students at City High spoke with pride about the status of their school, which the community widely regarded as the premier high school for blacks preparing to enter college. Put differently, the leadership and support within the black community deliberately fostered high academic expectations for this school's students. A large majority of graduates from City High went on to attend elite schools such as Howard, Yale, and Harvard Universities, whereas few from Neighborhood School did so.

How is it that City High was able to overcome many of the pernicious effects of discrimination whereas Neighborhood High actually reproduced them? I suggest that the key difference is in the high quality of leadership exhibited by inner-city school professionals as well as the exemplary level of community support engendered by such leadership. In other words, *principals and teachers took deliberate, affirmative steps to help make low-income black students academically and socially successful.*

In subsequent chapters, I will describe in detail strategies that all school leaders—principals, staff, teachers, and parents—can take in various contexts to achieve similar results. But first I must define a second pervasive type of discrimination uncovered through my research, *identity discrimination.*

Identity Discrimination

A result of the hidden curriculum in public schools enrolling large percentages of ethnic minority students is discrimination against students' identity (Mirón & Lauria, 1995; Troyna & Hatcher, 1991). This form of discrimination expresses itself through the tendency of (mostly white) teachers to associate low-income Latino and African American students with gangs and violence.

Gangs do exist in many cities and suburbs, and violence has become a way of life in some communities. What is often overlooked, however, is that leaders in some minority communities estimate that gangs and violent crime are attributable to only 2% of minority youth. According to leaders in the Chicano community, 98% of Chicano youth are innocent of violent crime. The even more telling statistic in, for example, places like Los Angeles County, is that Latino and African American youth also account for approximately 95% of the *victims* of violent crime, either as deliberate targets of criminals or innocent bystanders killed or injured by drive-by shootings (Allen, 1995, p. 13).

Fear of violent crime at school, therefore, appears to be fueling campaigns from organizations such as the American Federation of Teachers to make classrooms safer. Put simply, the continual airing on television of crime stories in minority communities contributes to the irrational fear among many teachers and principals that *most* poor ethnic minority youth are potentially violent criminals.

Even though this fear is understandable, we must work to eliminate it. As educators and citizens, we often deny that racial discrimination is both a cause and an outcome of the misrepresentation of minority students. But students are aware of this identity discrimination. Let's listen to N.B., an African American male at Neighborhood High.

> Some teachers have their favorites, but it ain't racism. She [my teacher] thinks that I'm a hoodlum. She thinks every black male she sees dressed like me is a criminal. It's something in the style of clothing that she considers them a hoodlum or gang member. A lot of [other] teachers say that, though. I hear them say that. (Lauria, Mirón, & Dashner, 1994, p. 25)

Effects of the Hidden Curriculum

Educational theorists have established many different kinds of curriculum. The two general kinds that we are interested in here are the formal (taught) and the hidden (informally learned) curriculum (Anyon, 1980; Apple, 1985; Jackson, Boostrom, & Hansen, 1993). The hidden curriculum is exemplified by behaviors, attitudes, and moral values that students informally, but systematically, learn in school. In this way, students learn important messages about life from principals, teachers, classroom routines (speaking in turn), and school policies. For example, teachers do not include the study of high moral content in their daily plans, but they inevitably pass on this knowledge to students.

Because many schools throughout the United States are located within or near dangerous neighborhoods, school personnel spend a lot of time making schools safer. For some students, the school is the only sanctuary from violence, poverty, and despair (Anfara, 1995). Like many other public institutions, schools also try to shelter youth from the dangers and temptations of the street. For example, nonprofit organizations, such as Community United for Fullerton Safety (CUFFS, 1996), are devoted to keeping "at-risk" students from joining gangs by offering enriching after-school activities and positive role models to "save" these youngsters.

This societal goal of rescuing youth from gang violence spills over into the classroom. Students told us that teachers frequently warned them that they would probably not graduate from high school, that they would in all likelihood become criminals. Realizing that there are more black males in prison than in college, and knowing that the dropout rate approaches 50% in large, urban school districts, teachers perhaps were advocating "tough love." Unfortunately, students' self-esteem often suffered as a result of this type of informal influence. And other teachers simply gave up on their students. Let's listen to A.H.:

> I know a boy that's graduating now who can't read. And they [his teachers] are not helping him by letting him go on. It's going to be hard for him to get a job. He's not going to be able to take care of himself. I mean I feel like that they [most teachers] only care about themselves. If they cared about their students, they wouldn't put up with half of the stuff that they do with them. They would let them know that they have a big world out there. You have to do what you have to do. If it takes for them to sit down and talk to the students and tell them how hard it is [out in the world], well let them do that. I don't know. I guess they are only looking out for themselves. (Lauria, Mirón, & Dashner, 1994, p. 26)

A consoling aspect of these interviews is that students often *did* believe in themselves. That is, they resisted the tendencies of some teachers and principals to regard them as potential gang members. At times, they valiantly fought the discriminatory effects of the hidden curriculum, which in its most pernicious form reproduced academic failure.

A major problem educators face is that students often perceive that they are struggling alone. Their parents are often overwhelmed and frequently jobless. My objective in this book is to suggest strategies that support students and help overcome discrimination in your school. But first I need to complete the summary of our research.

On the positive side, our research indicated that students can draw upon family and community support to overcome societal stereotyping and the low expectations of teachers. For Latino students, these types of support include a strong family and a keen desire to succeed in school. For some African American students we interviewed in the South, especially those at Neighborhood High, a sense of entitlement to quality public education as their *civil right* helped them make demands of their teachers and principals.

On the pessimistic side, teachers, perhaps out of fear, often gave up on students. Rather than "push out" students from high school, they simply passed them on to the next grade level, apparently without even the basic skill of reading (Fine, 1991; Weis & Fine, 1993). It is very unlikely that these students would go on to college. More probable is that they would fall prey to the underground economy of drug dealing in economically and socially distressed neighborhoods. More tragically, like the character "Strike" in the recent Spike Lee film, *Clockers*, these high school dropouts may well wind up indirectly contributing to murder and literally fighting for their lives in the streets of New York, Los Angeles, New Orleans, and Denver. Discrimination against students' identity, coupled with low academic expectations, may become a dramatic self-fulfilling prophecy. I emphasize the word *may* because it is my goal that this book assist school leaders—teachers and principals in both public and private schools—to take affirmative action along with the school community to prevent such a tragedy.

In summary, our data showed that discrimination is pervasive in a large number of schools and classrooms. Indeed, public laws and legal discourse notwithstanding, poor Latino and African American students experience discrimination because of their culture, language, and heritage. On the other hand, many Vietnamese students in the deep South and in communities like Irvine, California, are expected to graduate with honors.[3] I am very confident in the credibility of the data, that is, in the quality of information that students from neighborhood and magnet schools reported. Giving principals and teachers the benefit of the doubt, I believe that these school leaders follow the *letter of the law*. Principals promulgate school policies that prohibit discrimination; teachers' instructional practices attempt to "treat all students equally." I can only conclude that the hidden curriculum is largely responsible for discrimination in schools. It is a great challenge to uphold the *spirit of racial equality* that exists even beyond the law.

Social forces outside of schools, for example, those who want to make streets safe and bring jobs to communities, place tremendous pressure on schools to rid themselves of these ills. I hope to convince you of the need to accomplish a completely different goal: Schools must assist society by first ending their own pervasive discrimination, racism, and prejudice. Only then will we as citizens witness a healthy civil society.

Values and the Leadership Process

The leadership process is about taking action. In particular, leadership involves the affirmation of values. It goes without saying that in a democratic society, which embraces the values of equality, equity, and the full right of participation in civil society, pervasive discrimination "gets in the way." Schools are institutions that simultaneously mirror the qualities of the wider society and, through their function of education, may exercise leadership in shaping society. I view the leadership process in public schools as "moral politics" (see Maxcy, 1995a; Mirón & Elliott, 1994). Through the strategy of building effective student, governmental, and community partnerships, I believe public schools can rid themselves of discrimination and racism. The unique configuration of each school, owing to diverse social contexts, has resulted in institutions that are societies unto themselves. Thus if we in the research community and you as school leaders work to eliminate discrimination in the approximately 50,000 school districts throughout this country, it is conceivable that we can significantly transform or eliminate discriminatory practices throughout the United States.

Broadly conceptualized, there are two types of leadership strategies that we might build upon: (a) those that exist within the school community and (b) those that exist in the surrounding neighborhood and in the wider political community. Principals and teachers have vast experience applying "cooperative strategies" (Blase, 1991) inside the school building. For example, under the rubric of school decentralization, school site councils can build effective coalitions to implement a literature-based reading program and other forms of "whole language" instruction. These "inside" school partnerships are usually inspired by the vision of the school leader, usually the principal.

The cooperative "political" strategies I have in mind, however, emphasize affirmative action steps to achieve the unrealized promise of democracy. Of necessity, these coalition-building strategies stretch current democratic practices in schools by relying mostly on "bottom-up" maneuvers and what I term "horizontal" actions. They are simultaneously aimed at equalizing power relations within the school, furthering the postmodern tenet that *no one individual need be in charge all of the time*. This perspective on the leadership process, for example, emphasizes the *process values* of critical pragmatism (Maxcy, 1995a, 1995b). We need to rethink the idea that some individuals lead while their followers get rewarded.

As outlined in subsequent chapters, teacher-initiated cultural inquiry and student-led governance in public schools (see Apple & Beane, 1995) are effective concrete models used to illustrate positive affirmative steps within schools. Outside the school community, the untapped resources of local government, community-based organizations such as the Boys' and Girls' Clubs, and human relations commissions powerfully complement the academically inspired coalitions inside the school. Successfully negotiated, the postmodern leadership process I advocate—and will detail in the succeeding chapters—can further the twin goals of resisting discrimination and building reconceptualized school-community relations. Local communities can then be nurtured and enhanced, perhaps even stimulating the wider civil society to become a place that all of us can speak of with pride.

The ultimate goal, as Fukuyama (1995) reminds us, is to forge meaningful relationships within and outside of the school to create a climate of trust. It is my strong belief that only through superior relationships can civil society in the United States safely embrace the values of diversity and differences.

Notes

1. In California, the passage of Proposition 187 (1994) denied illegal immigrants entry to public schools. However, numerous organization representing ethnic minority groups have filed suit to overturn this initiative. Compounding the problem is the passage of Proposition 209 on November 6, 1996. This proposition makes it illegal to consider race and gender in hiring practices and in college and university admissions standards. This in fact nullifies affirmative action in California.

2. Student teachers' anecdotal evidence collected in Southern California schools indicates similar findings, especially among lower-income Latino students.

3. The Vietnamese example is an analytically separate and delicate case with its own set of problems which are, unfortunately, not within the scope of my research.

How Leaders Can Prepare for Action

Chapter 1 demonstrates that discrimination pervades classroom life in schools. Students interviewed seem caught in conflict between their faith in school policies that purport to prohibit racial discrimination and their experience of unequal academic treatment and prejudice against who they are. It doesn't matter if these are "merely" student perceptions. If African American and Latino students perceive that their white classmates have a better chance at making higher grades, and thus are discouraged or engage in counterproductive behaviors of resistance, then we must address these concerns. This chapter details the steps and values principals and teachers can affirmatively invoke to begin preparation for action.

Leadership is a process. As such, it embraces a set of moral-ethical values and administrative procedures that link goals and objectives to meaning and purpose. According to Maxcy (1995a, 1995b), the process values school leaders (including teachers, students, and principals) can summon to take moral action fall into three categories: (a) communication; (b) aesthetic intelligence; and (c) community. These values enable school leaders to link their decisions and actions to a moral purpose, such as ridding a school of discriminatory practices. Coupled with the use of practical critique and judgment, these types of values are substantive tools with which leaders can equip themselves to resist discriminatory practices in schools.

11

Opening Communication

Ridding public schools of discrimination, as more than 200 years of U.S. history informs us, is not easy. Gone are the times when principals can simply dictate to teachers an instructional method or selection of textbooks. Similarly, teachers, if they expect to invite parents to their classrooms as meaningful "partners," must cope with demands that may seem far removed from daily lesson plans. Societal pressures to reinvent education make it less likely that autocratic decision making will be successful in schools that are increasingly characterized by diversity and difference.

Employing the process values of communication in schools is a path principals and teachers can take to move away from autocracy. As countless examples ranging from the breakup of the Soviet Union to the "Million Man March" have shown us, our world is ready to move on to a different social paradigm. According to Maxcy (1995a; also see Murry, 1995), three principles highlight the communication process in schools:

1. A continuous discussion and an openness to dialogue (ongoing conversation) and debate about school goals and the means to achieve them
2. "Discursiveness" (the use of language and ideas) that is intimately related to concrete school practice
3. A dialogue about the *technical mission* of the school (teaching and learning) that is concrete, conceptually cast, "critical" (looks beneath the surface), and accessible to all members of the school community, especially students and parents

Without two-way channels of communication, it becomes virtually impossible to mount affirmative attacks on thorny problems such as discrimination and racism in public schools. "Discursiveness is taken to be intimately connected to practice, rather than being antecedent to practice" (Maxcy, 1995a, p. 129). Principals must communicate with teachers the reasons behind their decisions if they expect these decisions to have an impact. As curriculum leaders, teachers must communicate with students (and also with principals) the relevance of subject matter. No communication, no meaningful action!

Communicating Values

According to Starratt (1991, 1994), leadership is marked by *substantive* rationality as well as instrumental rationality (Weber, 1968). This distinction emphasizes the likelihood that in order to make a difference in the lives of the principal clients of the school, students, parents, and school administrators together must negotiate meaning with the school community. Why is achieving meaning in the school important? How can principals "negotiate" meaning?

Corporate leaders like to invoke two terms when embarking upon the complex tasks of strategic planning. These are *mission* and *vision*. The mission of an organization engulfs a strategic aim. That is, it has to do with the operational focus and relatively narrow scope of activities that enable the organization to become successful. Two immediate examples come to mind. First, a business obviously must find its niche in the market in order to make a profit and continue to survive—that is, remain competitive. Second, schools must, at least in the short term, attend to their instructional purpose and focus on student achievement.[1]

I do not wish to be misunderstood here. Schools are *not* corporations. They do not exist to make a profit. However, like businesses, schools are social organizations whose principals and teachers strive to instill a sense of community. As such, schools have a purpose, a mission. The vision of the school, on the other hand, is a portrait of its ideal future. By narrowing its vision, any organization increases its chances of reaching its short- and long-range substantive goals.

What distinguishes the perspective I advocate here is that communicative values ultimately must move beyond statements about means and ends—teaching and learning. Some overriding sense of the future, some vision—for example, a social goal such as practicing racial-ethnic equality in the classroom—must underpin communication. Indeed, most of the empirical research on leadership has this point in common: The most technically successful organizations (whether for profit or not for profit), public interest enterprises, have successfully achieved a well-defined, shared vision. The leadership process, therefore, communicates meaning and purpose, a substantive vision of the school that concretely paints an artistic portrait of the future. The following philosophical principles can guide us in achieving meaning and purpose in public schools. Maxcy's second process value, aesthetic intelligence, is the tool we employ to achieve vision and an artful school environment in which to work.

Employing Aesthetic Intelligence

Placed within the perspective of school administration, aesthetic intelligence repositions practice as intellectual inquiry (Maxcy, 1995a). Traditionally, school administrators have relied on absolutes, a result of the idealistic belief in some singular universal "truth" (the vision of the principal or the mission of the school as printed in brochures). Principals, and at times classroom teachers, invoke rigid ideas, such as "mastery learning," to rationalize all actions. Such rituals foreclose two-way communication. The practice of two-way communication can be used, instead, to overcome institutional lethargy. In this section, I elaborate on another process value that assumes the tenets of participatory democracy in public schools: aesthetic intelligence.

If we emphasize *pragmatism* in actions that lead to direct, concrete results in daily life in our schools "we may never discover the ideal form of educational leadership and/or practice." However, through intellectual inquiry "members of the school community can continually search for better ways of governing themselves and educating students" (Murry, 1995, p. 96). Put differently, the use of aesthetic intelligence involves the continuous critical examination of school policies and administrative procedures, as well as the reconciliation of the broad vision of the school with its strategic aims (see Levin, 1988). In this way, students, teachers, and parents are free to engage in experimental ideas and strategies. Further, these leaders can focus on ends rather than on the technology of means (standardized tests). They might reject, for example, a universal, absolute school vision in favor of a dynamic, ongoing shared vision that still can be pragmatically oriented. If old policies do not work, then this type of leadership process ensures that we are free to move on.

Achieving a Shared Vision

What many of us have learned about the school restructuring movement is that shared governance works. By "works" I mean that it has pragmatic value. It makes a difference in the daily life of schools. Together principals and teachers can set a vision for the school, such as resisting and overcoming discrimination. And this is only the starting point. School leaders working collaboratively can then deliberately take steps to invite students and parents to join in a dialogue about the vision—warmly, and with care!

I caution that the major professional "actors" should offer the invitation warmly, because there is the potential for conflict in engaging the school community in this way. A common dialogue about the shared vision of the schools however, can be set up in such a way as to welcome practical criticism, discussion, debate, and reflection. But it must be out in the open. The current dialogue on racism in our society reflects what happens when there is a hidden agenda. Commenting on former head of the Joint Chiefs of Staff General Colin Powell's failure to take a position on the Million Man March in Washington, D.C., journalist Dan Schnur (1995) writes:

> [Powell's] reaction to the Million Man March has been a study in risk-aversion. He did not attend the march, initially explaining his absence not on principle but on scheduled conflicts. He carefully walked both sides of the [racial] divide, gingerly embracing the march's ideals while distancing himself from its organizers. (p. B9)

Including Everyone

Failure to take a stand on discrimination in public schools is a failure to set a shared vision that nurtures minority students. The reason is simple. If both teachers and administrators responsibly set forth a vision, then of necessity no individual student will be excluded. We can trust teachers to paint an ideal portrait of the school that works for all children! Brought into the leadership process through two-way communication, teachers are then free to think of their students, especially the disadvantaged ones. On the other hand, if principals defy contemporary logic and systematically exclude teachers or, worse, manipulate them into thinking that their voices will be heard, teachers will respond accordingly. They will be programmed to ignore the needs of students, perpetuating academic discrimination and the stereotyping of ethnic minority students as potential gangsters or hoodlums.

With a broader perspective, schools can become successful organizations when leaders work to communicate purpose and meaning that includes all members of the community. This hypothesis does not imply that routine administrative procedures are inconsequential. To the contrary, when tied to the emerging *new* culture of the school that a shared vision engenders, standard operating procedures assume even greater relevance. This is so because teachers, and hence students, who before were excluded from the larger aims of schooling or, more subtly, were asked to "buy in" to a supposed vision through cooperative strategies (Blase, 1991), are now integral to the leadership process. In this manner, principals can negotiate meaning with teachers. By extension, teachers can help students construct the meaning of school life and welcome parents as true partners into their classrooms.

Experiencing Community

The Making of Meaning

I have written extensively about schools as multiple social constructions of reality (Mirón, 1996; Mirón & Lauria, 1995). Simply stated, people define the realities of schooling, which of necessity get renegotiated and redefined in varying social contexts. It is the context embedded in school structures, therefore, that largely shapes what actions principals and teachers can take to combat discrimination (Giddens, 1986; Starratt, 1994). As I have previously argued (Mirón, 1996), structures do not dictate what can be done. *Individuals* make the decisions that result in school policies and state laws. Individuals, therefore, can change such rules to favor the affirmative steps needed by their school community.

School leaders renegotiate meaning by altering structures—policies, rules, procedures, staffing configurations. Teachers and principals start with students and then reach out to parents and other members of the community. I detailed in earlier sections of this chapter how "substantive rationality" can be invoked to achieve purpose and meaning. In schools, we call this process setting a vision, which includes the core principle of critical pragmatism: participatory democracy. Only by preparing to create democratic institutions bent on achieving high levels of moral development can we hope ever to rid our schools of discrimination. The ultimate test of a school vision, Sergiovanni (1994) might argue, is a school's sense of community held together by shared values but constantly renewed and energized by democracy.

Community as Participatory Democracy

I use the term *community,* following Sergiovanni (1994), as a set of shared values that members of an institution or geographic space employ to work toward common goals. Within the perspective of school-community relations, I define the *local community* to mean those residents who are bound together by neighborhood and an interest in preserving their quality of life.

The process value of community represents the organizational context through which the rigidity of bureaucracies such as public schools can be mediated. We need a mechanism in public schools to deal effectively with the chaos in the local community as well as the wider society. I mean that students, teachers, and principals—working together—can redesign schools to provide sanctuaries from the perils of crime, poverty, and violence. This does not mean, however, that schools are to abdicate their responsibility to improve the quality of local life. To the contrary, the move to improve schools from within increases the potential for a better society. This paradox is dramatically illustrated by the efforts public schools have already taken to eradicate the twin ills of discrimination and racism. We can begin this long journey by establishing communities inside the school. Maxcy (1995a) argues:

> [School] communities have as their goal individual human beings participating and providing mutual recognition. Through the everyday practice of dialogue, conversation, phronesis (practiced wisdom), practical discourse, and judgment, the goal of community solidarity and unity would be sought. (p. 68)

The desired end of the process value of community is deep participatory democracy. Yet schools can embrace democratic values, such as allowing all voices to be heard and consensus building, only to the extent permissible under state law and local policies. The outdated adage that schools "were not meant to be practicing democracies" is all too frequently invoked even today. In order to prepare for community building, the following guidelines are recommended.

1. School leaders need to listen actively to clients and community members.

2. School leaders should view their role as one of service (see Beck, 1994).

3. Teachers are to be sensitive when handling the uninformed learner.

The strategic emphasis here is placed upon meeting collective needs as opposed to catering to individual egos or self-aggrandizement. Although individual students certainly merit attention, the effectiveness of a school community is ultimately determined by the extent to which the school as a shared culture is a happy place to learn, work, and make a contribution.

In summary, the process values of communication, aesthetic intelligence, and community redirect school leaders' attention away from technical rationality, or the pursuit of "efficiency," and toward the fulfillment of meaning—that is, toward substantive rationality. Furthermore, these three values are intertwined. Two-way communication ensures that language and ideas are not subordinated to decisions ("quick fixes"). Aesthetic intelligence focuses the content of communication in schools on the discovery of new approaches (structures and policies) that are tied to artful appreciation of everyday life.

Finally, the experience of community helps realize what is critically missing in schools: meaningful democratic practice. I next illustrate with concrete examples from practice how there can be no deep habit of discrimination when schools embrace the values of the authors of the U.S. Constitution. I use case-study data from two schools that experimented with the values of participatory democracy through the Accelerated Schools Process (ASP; see Hopfenberg, Levin, & Chase, 1993).

How Values Affect Outcomes

The Accelerated Schools Approach

In the mid-1980s, Henry Levin and his colleagues at Stanford University began experimenting with the idea that "at-risk" students could benefit from the same instructional programs that had traditionally served gifted and talented students. An economist by training, Levin recognized the devastating impact on the economy that declining academic achievement among low-income, minority students was having. His concern was that these students would not attain the skills needed to secure employment in a global economy.

Levin envisioned a society torn apart by economic and social inequality. He pointed to the telling statistic that "at-risk" students often would fall as much as 4 years behind their counterparts by the time they reached the eighth grade. (Levin, 1988; Mirón & St. John, 1996). Remedial education, with its watered-down "pull-out" instruction, was the culprit. The long-term solution was to systematically implement "accelerated learning" in public schools across the country.

In 1990, the University of New Orleans selected two neighborhood elementary schools as pilot sites for the Accelerated Schools program. A university-based facilitation team selected these schools, located in lower- and middle-class African American communities, based upon proposals submitted by school committees and the recommendations of the central office. "School A" was headed by an African American woman principal and was located in a demographically changing middle-class community near the university. The principal of "School B," a white British male, was trained in the "open classroom" methods in England. Both student bodies were majority, if not fully, African American. Both leaders were enthusiastic about the possibilities of introducing powerful learning strategies, such as whole language, in the everyday practices of their schools. Both publicly, and through their written applications and personal interviews, endorsed the democratic principles and shared governance of the Accelerated Schools Process. The two principals, however, showed radically different philosophies when it came to acting on values.

School A

The following anecdotes illustrate how a principal's attitude and commitment can affect the implementation of the values of participatory democracy in schools. At School A, the principal unconsciously applied Maxcy's process values described above. She listened attentively to the recommendations of her curriculum and parental involvement committees (composed of teachers and a university facilitator). For example, she waited before embarking hastily on implementing an Afrocentric curriculum centered on the creative arts and dance. She specifically asked to be put on the curriculum committee and deeply believed in the capacity of the arts to make a difference in student achievement for her mostly African American students. She also waited patiently so as to let trust develop among the faculty. Soon the staff recognized that she was serious about teacher empowerment.

Parental involvement at her school, at least among mothers, was not bad in comparison to other mostly black neighborhood schools in New Orleans. Mothers routinely dropped off their children at school, then remained to talk with teachers. Even so, teachers remained skeptical about the efficacy of parental involvement because those parents who liked to "hang around" did not offer to assist in classroom tasks such as running off ditto sheets.

One of the parents volunteering consistently in the school was the father of a second grader and a leader in the local community. He had dreams of starting a "Dads' Club." Astutely, he influenced the parental involvement committee to sponsor a get-acquainted social where a special effort was made to get fathers to attend. The event drew more than 100 parents in a school with about 500 students! Astonishingly, about 50% of the attendees were fathers. This positive turnout not only refuted some of the myths about the "absent father" in the black community, but it also convinced teachers that, with a little encouragement, parents could be brought in as partners in the classroom.

School B

At School B, the principal could not let go of administrative control. He espoused the values of participatory democracy, and teacher empowerment in particular. However, at every turn he rebuffed the recommendations of his teacher-led task forces. For example, it was 6 months before he accepted the vision statement his teachers had hammered out. In meetings with the university facilitation team, the principal acknowledged that he had rejected both the global vision statement and the specific curriculum recommendations because they were not "child centered." He complained that the process the teachers employed was not substantive and that the teachers did not fully understand the principles and methods of the ASP. He was not an active participant in the work of the committees, failing to observe one of the first principles of participatory democracy.

Using Process Values to End Discrimination

Uncovering Racial Issues

As a society, we are in heavy denial about discrimination and racism. As a profession, we naively believe that our school policies protect students from discriminatory practices that may harm them academically or, worse, damage their self-esteem for years. We can do something affirmatively at both levels. The two case vignettes described above, when probed critically, reveal deep underlying racial conflicts.

At School A, the female African American principal implemented the ASP at a time when the New Orleans public schools experienced the worst strike in the district's history. School A employed a biracial faculty of which approximately 70% were African American and 30% were white. The strike split along the racial divide. Virtually all of the African American faculty chose to walk the picket line. Almost no white faculty joined them. The faculty who chose to report to work, and continue the ASP, left school in others' automobiles because some of the striking faculty punctured holes in their tires! However, the principal did not attempt to punish the striking faculty members, who had widespread community support in the face of a recalcitrant school board.

Rather, the principal hired a human resources consultant with experience in conflict resolution, team building, and strategic planning. The consultant presented a series of staff development workshops principally designed to "lend voice" (Weis & Fine, 1993) to both the (mostly black) striking faculty and the (mostly white) nonstriking faculty. The principal felt that if the two sides were given the opportunity to air their differences, the school as a whole could get reunited, get back on task, and move on with the full implementation of the ASP.

Not one teacher mentioned the strike. Skeptics might wonder whether the faculty was intimidated by the format and chose to remain silent. However, the principal, focusing on the needs of students and the desire to give all voices the opportunity to be heard, did not attend the sessions. Also, the university facilitation team, including me, warned that any perceived preemptive move by the principal possibly would mean more than the end of a worthwhile experiment in empowerment and participatory democracy. It could possibly end her tenure at the school where she had been principal for 11 years. She listened to both her biracial faculty and the university team. She simultaneously embodied all of the three process values of communication, aesthetic inquiry, and community. Unfortunately, the reverse is true of the principal at School B.

At School B the principal did more harm than simply not listening to teachers and parents. He failed to respect them. The university facilitation team in which I participated observed a glaring example of the failure to respect teachers and African American culture. During Multicultural Week, which in black New Orleans schools often is cause for celebrating African culture, the principal chose instead to hang posters of Japanese art in the halls. In fairness, to hang posters of Japanese culture and art is not morally wrong when approached decontextually. However, when this behavior is placed in the social context of this neighborhood school in a low-income, all-black neighborhood in New Orleans, the behavior is unacceptable. It only added fuel to the brewing fire of racial conflict between the white principal—and his support group of white teachers—and the black teachers and parents who suspected that he was racist. Whether accurate or not, teachers, parents, and neighborhood residents concluded that the principal was racist.

Involving Parents

Racial issues, pervasive in some neighborhood schools in this country, signify an important dimension in the practice of participatory democracy in public schools: *community empowerment.* Each faculty member in our two cases identified parental involvement as a major challenge in the "taking stock" process (Hopfenberg, Levin, & Chase, 1993). As mentioned above, the activities of the parental involvement task force at School A seemed to make a lasting difference by helping fathers form a "Dads' Club" to help care for the school's physical plant. Also, an ongoing group of 30 volunteers (mothers, fathers, neighborhood residents, even a few grandmothers) formed to assist teachers in the classroom and to support financial needs. For example, the group raised money to supplement the school's air-conditioning fund.

Lewis and Nakagawa (1995) argue that class and racial variables profoundly shape the two principal forms of parental involvement in public schools toward either "enabling" or "empowering" models of participation. *Enabling* parents assume more superficial support activities such as raising funds. *Empowering* parents play major policy roles such as involving themselves in curriculum development.

Clearly, School A exhibited strong tendencies toward enabling models. The fact that the dads' activities were confined to volunteer labor, and that the teachers recruited mothers to assist them as volunteer aides, lends evidence to this view. Had the parental advisory task force *not* chosen to reach out to the black fathers, the stereotypical portrait of their "absent" parenting would have perpetuated. In my experience, these dedicated men powerfully symbolized care, first to their own children, and, secondly, to all of the children at School A. The principal's active support of their efforts—including freeing up money to recognize their contributions at a Christmas banquet—was central to this unique experience of community in this neighborhood school.

At School B, the principal almost sabotaged the activities of the parental advisory committee. Almost. He resisted the move toward shared governance by refusing to delegate authority to teachers, and of course parents, in the proposed school council. After much prodding from the university facilitation team, the principal consented to sponsor a "Welcome Breakfast" for parents. The outing had a reasonable turnout. However, even the most involved parents were keenly aware of the escalating racial conflicts between the white principal and the black faculty. This division proved to be a reflection of wider racial and ideological conflicts between the school and the local community. As a community, the school was unable to overcome these wide differences during the life of the ASP.

This frustration led to the demise of the ASP at School B. The principal suspended the program under pressure from Stanford University and the sponsoring corporation. Thereafter, community pressures forced his resignation, which was significantly intertwined with the termination of the ASP.

The teachers at School B had viewed the implementation of the ASP as a commitment to teacher empowerment—in other words, to democratic principles and practices in their neighborhood school.

When the principal abused the program, parents supported the ASP and united behind the teachers. By squelching teacher, and hence community, voices, the principal paradoxically mobilized teachers, parents, and neighborhood residents against him. He eventually was removed from the school.

Taking action in concert with community groups and parents can be a tricky business. In particular, when the organizational context encourages teacher empowerment, inevitably there will be disagreements between professionals (teachers) and citizens (parents and neighborhood residents). Taking action on values—the hallmark of leadership in public schools—involves taking risks. There is, quite simply, no alternative to taking risks when tackling the thorny problems of discrimination and institutional racism.

Note

1. In the long term, schools in urban contexts in particular need to "redraw boundaries" and assist in local community development. See L. F. Mirón (1995), "Pushing the Boundaries of Urban School Reform: Linking Student Outcomes to Community Development," *Journal for a Just and Caring Education*, 1(1), 98-114.

What Administrators Can Do

In the previous chapter, I analyzed the leadership process, linking leadership in schools to the presence or absence of institutional discrimination and racism. Such leadership is generally about "acting on values" concerning the problems of everyday life. The remainder of this book addresses issues of practice, especially how various forms of leadership, ranging from the administration of schools to collaboration with political leaders, can be invoked to rid public schools of pervasive discriminatory practices.

Bridging Community and Curricula

The multicultural curriculum is a popular vehicle with which to embrace diversity in public schools. When students and teachers learn to appreciate the contributions of nonwhite people to U.S. culture in the areas of art, history, literature, math, and science, a more welcoming school climate can result. By studying multicultural art and literature, one can see that there exist both "collective" and individualistic approaches to cultures. Thus school administrators will be motivated to work not only with students but also with entire families to support the teaching and learning goals of the school.

Instituting a multicultural curriculum as an "add-on" is usually insufficient (Banks, 1988). For example, limiting school appreciation of other cultures to celebrations of important holidays (e.g., Cinco de Mayo) or occasional activities, such as the sharing of ethnic foods, does not substantially alter a community's fundamental attitudes toward people, much less change its behavior. In other words, we can institute multicultural practices in schools with much fanfare, yet continue academic and identity discrimination in our classrooms. Something more profound is needed. In the next section I describe how to reap benefits from working with the local community to implement an effective multicultural curriculum.

Developing a Community-Specific Plan

One of my former students, Louise Olsen, has been the principal of a multiethnic school in eastern New Orleans for more than a decade. Boré Elementary School enrolls approximately 65% Asian American students (Vietnamese, Laotians, and Mekong), 33% African American students, and 2% white or Hispanic students. The school is situated in a rapidly changing community in New Orleans, once the center of a thriving aerospace industry and later adopted by many Vietnamese and other Asian families as their second home in the wave of resettlement after the Vietnam War. The community is demographically unique in New Orleans but similar to many other cities in that the racial-ethnic conflicts and socioeconomic problems have spawned gang violence, occasionally marked by assassination-type killings.

Principal Louise Olsen recognized the emerging crisis as well as the untapped resources in her community. New Orleans is predominantly Catholic, as are many of the families at Boré Elementary, so Dr. Olsen began planning for a multicultural curriculum with the Catholic Church. The Vietnamese pastor of the congregation near the school was very supportive of the principal and supportive of public schools generally. Indeed, many of his parishioners attended the school because they couldn't afford even the comparatively modest cost of local parochial schools. Dr. Olsen asked the pastor to host community meetings with her, and several of her teachers agreed to participate in a steering committee to implement a multicultural curriculum that would be sensitive to community needs.

The principal employed the techniques of "participatory (action) research" (Anderson, Herr, & Nihlen, 1994) while maintaining her traditional leadership role. That is, she formed several teacher-led committees to both survey the needs of the Asian community and devise strategies to introduce a multicultural curriculum to ethnic minority students as a group without ignoring individual needs. The idea was to alert the other "minority" students (blacks and whites) to the presence of the area's non-European culture. The principal wanted to build an awareness of the discrimination felt by students and families who live on the margins of American society. It was a concept not widely accepted in a school district controlled largely by African Americans, many of whom had earned their stripes fighting on behalf of civil rights in racially divided New Orleans.

Selecting a Meeting Place

The first step toward the goal of implementing a multicultural curriculum sensitive to community needs was to pick a meeting place. Dr. Olsen chose the local Catholic church. This move was risky because not all of the Asian families were Catholic, and certainly the majority of the other students were of other religious denominations. Nevertheless, the church proved a good choice for meetings because of its proximity to the school. Also, the pastor was highly regarded as a leader by the local Vietnamese-speaking community. The school enrolled large numbers of Vietnamese families who lived, sometimes two families together, in low-income, federally subsidized apartments in the area.

I cannot overemphasize the significance of selecting the church as the initial meeting place in this particular situation. The connections between low-income, government-subsidized apartments and the social isolation of the Vietnamese students became increasingly evident (Garvin, 1994). Eastern New Orleans had developed a reputation among middle-class homeowners (both white and black) as a place that harbored apartment residents who apparently lacked a respect for private property. Thus there was already an existing bias against the students and their parents who lived in these government-subsidized apartments. As a leader of the families, the Vietnamese pastor was able to command respect from his parishioners. Equally important, he could help mediate any social conflict between middle-class homeowners and low-income renters. He proved to be an important ally for the principal.

Defining the Issues

What are the prevailing issues of different minority groups within the local community? What conflicts are apparent? Specifically, how can the principal negotiate meaning among the families and teachers that will simultaneously address issues in the local community and further the vision for a multicultural curriculum? These are questions that all administrators must face when planning changes that serve the entire community.

Dr. Olsen began with language. She discovered during the early brainstorming sessions that one of the *internal* conflicts across the Vietnamese families was the issue of literacy. Who could read and write among them, and among other ethnic groups, was a function of gender and social class. Not all Asian American families were poor or uneducated. In addition, many males had formerly held important military posts in Vietnam; one had even been a general in the Vietnamese army. Like many of his counterparts, he had been educated in France and spoke several languages, including English.

Many of the low-income mothers, on the other hand, not only did not speak English, but they also couldn't read or write in their native (Hmong) dialect. Unknowingly, the principal practiced a form of aesthetic intelligence when she targeted the inequitable relationships caused by differences in social class and language. She quickly observed that certain conflicts within the Vietnamese community were social class and gender-related issues. For instance, males, dominant in Vietnamese society, were clearly emerging as local spokespersons. Because of their enforced illiteracy, many of the mothers had been silenced (Weis & Fine, 1993) both linguistically and socially. They were unable to command social status in Vietnam or New Orleans and received little respect in the community as school partners.

To further her plan to create a shared vision in the community, the principal needed to resolve these issues. The *strategic* goal of developing a multicultural curriculum needed to be tied to the issues of *meaning* (Starratt, 1993, 1994) if the process value of communication was to take hold.

Taking Action

The principal next engaged in fairly standard team-building and strategic-planning techniques to discuss and debate the values of multicultural education and multiculturalism (Banks, 1988; Cortés,

1995). These included: a) dialogue exercises, b) information gathering, and c) reflection. The unusual fact was that, as part of the dialogue, the principal did not shun conflict. Indeed, she prepared her staff for it. "The differences between conflict resolution and consensus building were discussed, and the ground rules for the discussion were established" (Olsen, 1994, p. 151).

Most school restructuring models that attempt to build systemic change into the school culture focus on promoting a team spirit. For example, the Accelerated Schools Process relies extensively on team-building exercises to rally the members of the school community behind a single goal or narrow set of strategic priorities, such as the infusion of the arts across the curriculum (Dell, 1995). Even Comer's (1980) community-grounded model of school restructuring relegates parents to advisory (enabling) rather than policy (empowering) roles, thus avoiding potential professional conflict with the principal and teachers.

Conflict, however, is inevitably part of change (Apple & Beane, 1995; Ball, 1987). As educators, we are taught that the expression of conflict is negative. Serious conflicts in the school, such as verbal and physical fighting among students, are to be avoided at all costs. Yet comparative research has established that, in countries such as Japan, the culture of public schooling encourages "free expression" (Tobin, 1995). The theory is that children will grow up with less hostility if they are able to work out their aggression in a structured environment. In the culture of American schooling, we seem to find all sorts of techniques to squelch what may, in fact, be healthy adaptation to change. Certainly the introduction of a major change like multicultural education carries its share of the conflict that accompanies uncertainty (Giddens, 1991).

At Boré Elementary, the principal experienced conflict that stemmed from the multiethnic demographics among the faculty and the students as well as socioeconomic differences within a particular social group, as in the case of the Vietnamese parents. How did she let this natural expression of conflict play out without thwarting her goal of uniting the school in the ideals of multicultural education?

Facing Conflict in the Multiethnic School

Parents at Boré Elementary wanted to address the inequities within the Asian American community. As I mentioned, some Vietnamese parents, especially males who were highly educated or previously had held high-level military posts in Vietnam, were accustomed to being in charge. They felt their ideas were best for the community. The rest of the parents naturally resented this elitism and sought support by asking the principal to hold large open meetings. One parent verbalized the underlying divisions as well as the long-term goal of moving beyond fragmentation:

> We need to know more about one another. It's okay for the kids. They have this [awareness session]. What about the adults? After all, the kids go home in the evening. They don't hear the same thing at home that they hear in school. All of the groups need to be together. (Olsen, 1994, p. 155)

This parent recognized that there were divisions within the Vietnamese community. Such an obvious fact is often overlooked by many of us working in multicultural education. We tend to think that minorities constitute one unified "community." In fact, there are several distinct communities. Boré Elementary School is typical of school communities across the country where a multiplicity of languages are spoken. Dr. Olsen was fortunate to have Chapter I and Chapter II funding available because of her high percentage of low-income students. She used some of the money to finance translators in the meetings with the Parent Teacher Association (PTA). This process of translation took time and invariably caused frustration among several language groups. The African American parents, of course, spoke English. Also, the French-educated Vietnamese parents were fluent in English. However, the majority of the lower-income working-class Vietnamese parents, especially mothers, could not understand spoken English. They wanted translators.

Establishing Linguistic Equity

The principal describes the tedious process as follows. Initially, she employed three translators. One translator would be stationed before the group, next to the speaker. The English-speaking facilitator (the principal, a teacher, or an English-speaking Vietnamese parent) would talk for the equivalent of a written paragraph (about a couple of minutes). The translator would give that part of the presentation in Vietnamese. Obviously these sessions were quite lengthy.

Conflict among the English-speaking attendees ensued for two reasons. First, they did not need any translation and thus considered it a waste of time. Secondly, they felt excluded during the Vietnamese translations; they were not used to a subordinate linguistic position.

Dr. Olsen later observed: "Since Vietnamese pronunciation, enunciation, and intonations are very different from English, the audience sometimes perceived statements to be hostile even though they were not. This caused me some trepidation" (Olsen, 1994, p. 156). The team-building effort of the PTA was temporarily displaced in favor of linguistic-equity issues. When linguistically excluded groups began splintering among themselves, carrying on English conversations during the Vietnamese translations, the facilitator suggested that small-group discussions take place. Eventually the facilitator's suggestion became the compromise, even though this separation into groups by language had a somewhat divisive effect. Furthermore, the principal was unable to cover all of the material her steering committee had planned. Still, the formation of multiple groups seemed to be the most appropriate solution because it met the needs of the various language groups.

Allowing Parents to Facilitate

Parents, with the support of teachers and the principal, became the facilitators of the PTA meetings, which caused significant changes. These parents reworked the mission of the school. Moreover, they made important policy recommendations for the multicultural curriculum. They assumed empowering roles in curriculum development. Small discussion groups of parents and community representatives, who had been ill at ease in the large group format, began meeting regularly.

The parent groups discussed their expectations for the school. The discourse focused on how the traditional academic structure (the 8:00 a.m.–3:00 p.m. schedule; the European-centered curriculum; pull-out English as a Second Language classes) did not meet their children's needs. Furthermore, because parents worked long hours and had no private transportation, they wanted the staff to care for their children after school. The school did not have a budget for an after-school program, so the principal and teachers used parent volunteers to achieve the goals of their community-specific curriculum.

Curriculum-development teams met at the school and included teachers and parents working collaboratively. During the curriculum-development process, each team met three times for no less than 3 hours each session. Each group reviewed the grade-level specifications of the written curriculum guidelines as promulgated by the school district and the state department of education. The standards of the written (published) curriculum were compared to the actual taught (hidden) curriculum in the classrooms. Of course there were discrepancies. The teacher-parent teams addressed these deviations, making certain that children were not tested at a higher grade level if the actual curriculum did not include the subject matter.

It was not easy to move Vietnamese parents, especially working mothers, into empowerment roles. The principal noted that Asian American parental involvement decreased during the implementation of the multicultural curriculum "from 40% to 10% participation" (Olsen, 1994, p. 187). Oftentimes, parents are part of a *home culture*, similar to Latino-Chicano culture, that relates all responsibility for schooling to teachers. There are steps, however, that can remedy this trend. Dr. Olsen discovered that issuing formal invitations to parents to visit the school was an affirmative step she could take. On the other hand, sending special invitations to Vietnamese families became a source of embitterment for many of the African American and white parents. Because these groups perceived that Vietnamese parents didn't help raise funds or participate in special school activities (such as staff development workshops for other ethnic groups), they felt discriminated against.

There was open conflict among the teachers, who experienced stress brought on by the Vietnamese parents' new empowerment role and the accompanying pressure for change. Olsen quotes one teacher's frustration with another faculty member's comments about her apparently traditional teaching methods:

> I remembered how I left your hall one day with tears in my eyes. I was determined you wouldn't know you had upset me. . . . But you attacked me . . ., made me feel like I hadn't done my job. . . . All I did was teach the children. . . . I can't perform miracles but I swore no one would know you made me feel like that. (Olsen, 1994, p. 190)

Moreover, the complexities and differences in the Asian community had become evident. The principal initially believed that a group of Laotian parents had dropped out of the planning and implementation process because of their respect for the professional autonomy and expertise of teachers and the principal. Deeper probing by the principal through interviews with community members revealed that this social group wanted to uphold the traditions of the farming culture in Laos wherein children typically assisted their parents with farming chores rather than attend school. Asians who fished in this South Louisiana region also were intimidated by the planning process. Class divisions seemed to further exacerbate cultural and social distinctions. For example, the fishermen were generally illiterate in both their native language and English.

When faced with cultural and socioeconomic facts, principals find that the ideal of parental empowerment becomes a two-edged sword. For the principal, who often provides administrative leadership to address discrimination, this realization of necessity means the adoption of multiple administrative roles.

Adopting Multiple Leadership Roles

During the complex process of planning and implementing an effective multicultural curriculum, Dr. Olsen experienced several changing leadership roles. Briefly stated, these included: a) instructional leader, b) curriculum developer, c) participant-observer (researcher), and d) nurturer of the vision.

At the conclusion of this chapter, I will specify other related leadership roles that principals can adopt when attempting to administer this type of curriculum while at the same time defining the issues of multiculturalism in the social and cultural context of the school (Cortés, 1995). Here I want to expand briefly upon the four leadership roles of the school administrator highlighted above.

The Administrator as Instructional Leader

The principal often must take the lead in keeping a school focused on its instructional mission. Multiple publics—parents, business leaders, politicians—demand accountability from administrators and staff to produce measurable results in achievement gains. These demands for academic accountability, in turn, have spurred school-reform movements such as Effective Schools and Success for All.

A paradox is likely to ensue, however. As calls for the professionalization of teaching intensify, teachers begin to resist intensified
monitoring of their instruction—often rightly so! The question facing all of us involved in implementing reform is: "Can we or can we
not trust teachers?" Continuous monitoring by administrators is
fundamentally incompatible with the concepts of teacher professionalism and empowerment. Public support of teacher empowerment,
along with the decentralization of decision making, which ultimately feeds teachers' desire to control the instructional program,
can undermine the strategies of school leaders (Wimpelberg, Teddlie, & Stringfield, 1989) and thereby thwart academic success for
students. Sometimes, the principal must switch roles in order to be
effective.

The Administrator as Curriculum Developer

An administrative leader who attempts to develop a multicultural curriculum is advised to play a collaborative role. Rather than
monitor teacher instruction or conduct summative evaluations
(Glickman, 1985, 1993), Dr. Olsen took a team approach. At Boré Elementary, she quickly formed discussion groups, first among faculty
and subsequently with parents, students, and community members.

In this case, it is difficult to assess the extent to which the collaborative process of curriculum development led to actual changes.
Clearly, the principal had a firm grasp of the direction in which she
wanted to move the school. She knew from experience that the old
Eurocentric curriculum was not working. However, she also wanted
to avoid the potentially devastating fragmentation that might result
from a curriculum that overly stressed "ethnic difference" (Mirón,
1996). By empowering all school stakeholders, both internal and external, she was able to ease discrimination while simultaneously creating a team spirit on behalf of multicultural education. Her vehicle
for realizing a shared vision was the curriculum. It soon became evident, however, that within the role of curriculum developer, the principal needed both to observe and to participate.

The Administrator as Participant-Observer

Perhaps the most difficult role of the collaborative leader is that
of participant-observer. A leader must study what needs to be done
in the school, much as an anthropologist investigates the values em-

bedded in the culture of a local community (Starratt, 1994). This observation necessitates research skills. As I will demonstrate in subsequent chapters, such skills are to be shared by administrators with the faculty, students, and parents. The traditional approach, however, has been to provide autocratic "quick fixes" to complex problems. Administrators have perceived that there is little time for reflective practice (Schon, 1983), much less for critical reflection (Freire, 1990). Yet both of these skills are *urgently useful* in the execution of the model I am proposing.

The key understanding is that the administrative leader in the school (principal, assistant principal, curriculum specialist) continues to be engaged in teaching *and* learning. Observation does not imply inaction. To the contrary, the postmodern perspective we advocate removes those sets of dualistic opposites—teacher versus leader, observer versus participant—that can hinder desired transformative change. As much poststructural theory informs us (Cherryholmes, 1988), there is no action apart from discourse-practice. And, observation, in our model, is a form of practice!

To observe astutely is also to communicate effectively about the content of one's observation. In the case study of two accelerated schools cited above, I noted that in School A, the principal voluntarily placed herself in the subordinate position as an equal member (*potentially*) of the curriculum cadre in the Accelerated Schools Process. However, in School B, the principal maintained administrative distance from the work of teachers, parents, and community members. Paradoxically, by not participating in the work of curriculum development—indeed, by participating merely by insisting on his desire for a child-centered program—he administratively controlled the process. I assert that this is a subtle yet pernicious form of academic and identity discrimination. In the case of School B, the principal's insensitivity and overt racism "disrespected" the African American culture of the school in the name of whole language, manipulative math, and other progressive reforms. On the other hand, by deferring to the needs of the teachers, School A's principal was able to gain long-term support for an Afrocentric program based on the performing and creative arts. She participated by listening.

The Administrator as Vision Keeper

Once the vision is a shared venture, nurturing it is relatively simple. Unlike the conflicting roles of participant-observer, the keeper of the vision role carries plenty of support. I caution that developing a shared vision is not a sales job. Part of cultural leadership (Bolman & Deal, 1991) is facilitating a shared vision among multiple stakeholders and partners. This is a bottom-up process that takes time.[1]

The administrative leader must resist the impulse to force a "buy-in." Adhering to Maxcy's (1995a) principles of communication and community, the principal should not seek an artificial consensus. Rather, through dialogue and debate, what I call a *consensus in process* will be the satisfactory result that slowly emerges.

Admittedly the role of vision keeper is a contradictory one. Although it may appear to be the job of just one person, it is not. The individual occupying a leadership position may be responsible for the ongoing process of emerging consensus related to policy and action. However, this activity need not be restricted to the principal. Indeed, as the practices of participatory democracy take root within the school community, and as local support for the global vision of the school grows, other leaders may arise to nurture the vision. This viewpoint may be unfamiliar to school administrators who have historically received training in preparation programs to function as managers (Rothstein, 1994). I will modify here a point I made in Chapter 2: Sustaining a shared vision in the school is part of renegotiating meaning. It is what brings life to schools as organizations and helps move them to assume the forms and practices of "community" (Beck & Foster, in press).

Equalizing Power Relations in the School Community

The various administrative roles described above point to a significant pattern—the successful leader moves to a less hierarchical position in the school organization. It is doubtful, however, that schools will actually be able to realize a shared vision, or other mechanisms of critical pragmatism, without serious attention to the inherently unequal power relations found there (Mirón, 1991). One would hope that, as the instructional leadership role moves from one of monitor to curriculum developer, a more collaborative relationship would naturally emerge.

As can be seen, the overall process is not easy. Administrators do not like to relinquish positions of power and control. By the same token, classroom teachers are in the habit of delegating responsibility over policy matters. In a hierarchy, these practices are understandable. In a community marked by collaborative leadership, however, they are unacceptable. Moreover, if the issue of unequal power relations is not given attention, as Sarason (1990) notes, school reform will fail altogether.

There is a two-edged sword in the process of conceptually moving schools from organizations to communities. Henry Levin (1988), founder of the Accelerated Schools Process, calls this challenge "empowerment coupled with responsibility." The scenario works like this. Administrative leaders must learn that they can more easily carry out their objectives for the school if they learn to give up administrative control. Paradoxically, when administrative control is relinquished, principals find it important also to share responsibility.

I want to avoid naiveté. This long, complex transition must avoid the pitfalls of "informal power sharing." By this I mean that eventually policy making must become formalized if shared decision making is going to work. Too often I have heard well-meaning experts on school reform simply respond that the process can work on an "informal" level. The process of power sharing may *begin* informally, but it must be institutionalized in public schools if teachers, in particular, are to take it seriously. Otherwise, school change will be perceived by principals and teachers as an extra burden. In a genuinely collaborative setting, professionals must be given formal authority for making decisions as well as the actual responsibility for doing the work.[2]

In summary, I have sought to be concrete about collaborative leadership roles within the school community. At first glance this sounds like an oxymoron. How can administrative leadership be collaborative? I believe it can if we pay serious attention to the equalization of power relations. Even though this task may not be easy, there are models based upon the informal sharing of power among administrators, teachers, parents, community members, and yes, even students. To be effective, these collaborative reform models must become institutionalized in the school. I end this chapter by listing the multiple administrative leadership roles possible within the school community. These roles are: (a) community relations specialist; (b) conflict resolver; (c) curriculum developer; (d) change agent; (e) resource seeker; and (f) culture builder (Olsen, 1994, pp. 266-282).

Notes

1. As my doctoral student, Steven Keller, principal of a middle school in Southern California, points out, this technique may not be suitable in "crisis situations." I acknowledge that sometimes democracy means being willing to make tough choices when students, teachers, or community members demand it. Such moments of crisis—for example, when schools are besieged by violence and crime—may, I hope, become the grist for the mill of reflection at a less stressful time.

2. Even when teachers and parents are given authority, problems may still result. For example, my colleague, Kathy Nakagawa, has studied the role of parents in the school site councils under the Chicago School Reform legislation. Here, parents were afforded the legal authority to hire and fire principals. However, many low-income minority parents did not receive adequate training and perceived their role as merely assisting the school. They did not envision their role as being policymakers. I have provided guidelines on how to handle both the "surface" (organizational) structure and the "deep" (race, gender, and class) structure. See L. F. Mirón, "The Dialectics of School Leadership: Poststructural Implications," *Organizational Theory Dialogue*, Fall 1991, pp. 1-4.

How Teacher Inquiry Can Serve Community

Chapter 3 described the sundry administrative leadership roles that support school action against discrimination. It incorporated case studies of two vastly different leadership philosophies. Furthermore, we saw that leadership processes are inseparable from instructional issues, both being of consequence in the effort to confront discriminatory practices and institutional racism in public schools.

Conducting Collaborative Research

This chapter presents an entirely different approach to dealing with discrimination in the classroom: *collaborative teacher research.* By "collaborative" I mean teachers working in teams, in concert with each other, with students, and with community groups. Much knowledge can be gained when administrative practices provide teachers with the time, energy, and support to conduct research on important issues facing students and their families.

Robert Bruesch is a sixth-grade teacher at Willard Elementary School in Rosemead, California, as well as a member of the city council. He holds beliefs in accord with an emerging body of literature that suggests that schools could be much more proactive than they presently are in shaping the quality of life in many areas: within the school, in the surrounding neighborhoods, and in the wider society

(Adler, 1996; Cole & Olt, 1994; Garvin, 1994; Mirón, 1996). Wearing unique "twin lenses" as classroom teacher and city councilman, Bruesch reflected on the loss of community in public schools:

> As a teacher and an elected official, I get to see the issues on both sides. I strongly feel we've lost a sense of community in the school. The people, the government structure, social agencies, seem to be working in a vacuum. What we need to do is to create alliances of community groups that meet the needs of the whole child. (Bruesch, 1995, p. B15)

A practical tool used to build community alliances is collaborative teacher research. In particular, teacher-initiated research that leads to identification and resolution of community-based problems helps restore community in the school. I call this type of research *action research* and recommend using this term despite some definitional problems.[1] If applied systematically, in concert with the needs of neighborhood residents and community members, action research is a powerful tool for empowering both classroom teachers and the students and families they serve (see Frederickson, 1995).

Appreciating the School as a Place for Inquiry

Classroom teachers are not accustomed to viewing themselves as researchers. Research is an activity that is conducted in universities and think tanks. Indeed, my experience working in teacher-preparation programs is that the research methods course, if it is required at all, is usually put off until the end of the program. Future teachers are understandably skeptical about a practice that carries an arcane image. Moreover, the "scientific," positivistic approach (Foster, 1986) discourages veteran teachers from acquiring the habits of inquiry out of lack of confidence (Hopfenberg, Levin, & Chase, 1993).

Conducting action research, however, is not about making scientifically valid claims. It concerns addressing the real everyday problems in public schools such as discrimination and institutional racism. Simply put, research that is conducted by the participants in the school (classroom teachers) is about making a difference in the everyday lives of students and their families. Above all, what makes action research possible in schools is a sense of urgency about the perceived or real crises facing the school community.

The key obstacle to developing innovative policies and procedures is lack of time. Organizational theorists and scholars in the politics of education write about the standard organizational routines that limit the time school professionals can spend on "development" as compared to "maintenance" activities (Peterson, 1981; Schlechty, 1990). In the two case studies presented in Chapter 3, however, the principals, despite their vastly different leadership philosophies, sensed a crisis. Thus, they found time during the school day to free up classroom teachers to embark upon a complex school-restructuring model, the Accelerated Schools Process (ASP).

The principal of School A grew increasingly disconcerted over data that indicated that *none* of her sixth graders had been accepted into a nearby magnet middle school the year before her school began the ASP program. At School B, the principal was under the directive of the Area Superintendent to raise test scores and improve discipline. He faced the loss of his job if he did not meet these goals.

Cultivating Attitudes for Action Research

In times of crisis, principals find ways to free up teachers to look for new approaches. This process involves research. What is more important, however, is the cultivation of a certain habit of mind. Schon (1983) describes the professional who develops a state of scholarly awareness as the "reflective practitioner." My proposal is to create a *collective* awareness among classroom teachers about the usefulness of action research. Changing the organizational culture of public schools to foster attitudes appreciative of research at the classroom and school levels requires a change in teacher roles.

I want to emphasize that, in order to cultivate a habit of inquiry in the classroom, teachers must view themselves as leaders in the school. For example, when developing a multicultural curriculum, principals cannot be expected to achieve this goal on their own. They need help. Classroom teachers are closest to understanding student needs and hence school families, thus they can most effectively generate the information necessary to plan and implement the curriculum.

The research process can work smoothly when the principal takes the lead in freeing up time for teachers. My conception, however, is that teachers are agents. They are able to act. Engaging in result-oriented, collaborative research is a form of what Jurgen

Habermas (1970) calls "communicative action." The results are collectively shared and frequently lead to concrete changes in school practice. It is also what John Dewey (1938) meant by "inquiry": the application of the scientific method.

As a form of communicative action, teacher research can lead to practical results. Working collaboratively on faculty teams or on teams consisting of faculty, students, and community members, teachers can cultivate a love of research as everyday practice. We need not wait for a crisis. In the remainder of this chapter, I will illustrate with examples from innovative teacher-preparation programs how the use of action research can help overcome identity and academic discrimination for Asian American, Latino, and multiethnic school populations.

Overcoming Asian American Stereotyping

Asian Americans: Minority Role Models?

In the summer of 1995, Suzi Charlton of the University of California, Irvine (UCI) and I supervised a pilot program of action research for beginning and future teachers. I say "pilot program" because as part of its certification in multicultural and bilingual education, the credential program at the university was experimenting with a form of teacher research called "cultural inquiry." The idea was that new teachers would volunteer in community agencies and not-for-profit organizations and engage in a form of descriptive ethnographic research to gain cultural knowledge of ethnic, linguistic, and racial minority groups in a context that was largely new to them. The teachers worked in heavily Latino inner-city schools in Santa Ana, California, as well as virtually intact ethnic minority communities like the Asian American community in Westminster, California, known as Little Saigon.

The overwhelming number of aspiring teachers responded far beyond our expectations. They were able to complete a fairly sophisticated assignment involving qualitative data collection and analysis (Spradley, 1979) in a 5-week institute format. But more significantly, they also established a number of interpersonal relationships with minority students whom they would otherwise not have had the opportunity to meet. I would like to summarize one of these research projects by three Asian American student-teachers who studied and analyzed "Asian Stereotypes."[2] In their introduction, the teacher-researchers articulated well the "double bind" many successful Asians experience in this country:

> Despite the many injustices Asian immigrants have endured and the severe hardships recent Asian refugees are currently undergoing in the United States, Asian Americans have seldom been viewed [by dominant groups] as an underprivileged minority who live under the same cloud of prejudice, discrimination, and hardship that other ethnic minorities do. Although Asians have had a history of oppression in the United States, their increasing affluence and educational attainments seem to belie the popular image of an oppressed and underprivileged subgroup. Rather, Asian Americans' apparently successful efforts at acculturation [and assimilation] into the dominant culture, believed by many to have been achieved with a minimum of discomfort, have earned them the dubious misnomer of the "model minority." (Chiu, Tron, & Chou, 1995, p. 1)

Targeting cultural conflicts. The teacher-researchers are quick to point out that, as with all stereotyping, there are elements of both truth and falsity embedded in our perceptions. Certainly many Asian American immigrants to the U.S. are hardworking and do well in school. The perception among many teachers that Asian families value a good education is confirmed in the interview data in the study cited in Chapter 1 (Mirón, 1996; Mirón & Lauria, 1995). Vietnamese students generally do well in school, but not all of them do. Some high-achieving Asian American students also pay dearly in emotional costs as a result of their double identities.[3] They honor their parents for the enormous sacrifices their parents make in putting them through school; at the same time, they face peer pressure to join youth gangs, just as other students do. The image of Asian students as a "model minority" is in reality a double-edged sword.

As the researchers point out, "groups that are not doing so well, such as the unemployed Hmong [see Chapter 3], the Downtown Chinese, the elderly Japanese, the Vietnamese gang members of Little Saigon, the older Filipino farm laborers, and others, have been rendered invisible" (Chiu, Tron & Chou, 1995, p. 4). Because of cultural differences, these groups experience substantial conflict on at least two levels: between Asian minority groups and the majority white culture; and within various Asian minority groups, especially those divided by "successful" and "nonsuccessful" classifications. The following excerpt from an interview with a Vietnamese elementary school student, Sandy, is telling: "Well, my parents tell me that I have to listen to adults, like teachers and stuff. I'm not supposed to talk too much, but I do anyway . . . and I'm supposed to listen to my parents, which is hard sometimes" (Chiu, Tron, & Chou, 1995, p. 8).

Cultural conflicts escalate when elementary students attend public schools that either undermine traditional Asian values (such as the tradition of not speaking back to adults) or overly stress American values that may conflict with those of Asian families. The researchers specify some of the American cultural norms that may cause this conflict, such as independence, assertiveness, and expressiveness (see also Tobin, 1995).

These conflicts obviously may affect a student's relationships with teachers. Also, the parents may begin to see marked changes in behavior at home as students become even more identified with the fabric of American school culture.

Sandy reveals her feelings about differences in cultures: "Sometimes it's hard, you know, to try to be Vietnamese and American at the same time. I get confused and I have to choose one or the other" (Chiu, Tron, & Chou, 1995, p. 9).

Myung Kim, a Korean American elementary student, expresses the tension somewhat differently:

I wish I could just let out what is bothering me sometimes. I'm an American so I should stand up for what I believe, but it's like I keep quiet and let it pass because that is what my parents tell me to do . . . I don't like the Asian way, but whatever. (Chiu, Tron, & Chou, 1995, p. 9)

Discriminating by language. The cultural conflicts reported in the interviews with elementary students come into sharp focus around language issues. Native language is the one dimension that most clearly defines a minority student's ethnic identity. Ethnic minority students and their families struggle to hold onto their native language and culture. This practice is often viewed as a sign of negative resistance to assimilation. In California, as in many states with large immigrant populations, there has been a political backlash against continued funding for bilingual education and other measures that purportedly delay the time needed for immigrants and naturalized minorities to learn and assimilate English.

Myung describes her struggle over language use at school and at home:

> If I were at school . . . with my friends, I would speak English, you know, act American. I think if I spoke Korean and acted in a Korean way at school, most kids would not see me as American, but probably as a[n] "FOB," you know, fresh-off-the-boat. But if I were at home with my family and relatives, I speak Korean and use my Asian side. If I don't, my family would say that I do not have respect for the Korean ways. (Chiu, Tron, & Chou, 1995, p. 10)

These interviews from Asian communities point to the value of collaborative research. Without the interviews it is doubtful that the teacher-researchers would know the full extent of cultural conflicts or the Asian students' struggle between the use of native and second languages. I observed the student teachers presenting their research findings to peers in the UCI Institute and witnessed the awe on the other future teachers' faces. Most of them had already accepted the stereotype of Asians as the "model minority."

The issue of language use is of particular importance to classroom teachers working to overcome discrimination. Unknowingly, teachers may foster discrimination in the wider society by an insistence on speaking English in the classroom. Well-intentioned, concerned by the possibility that their immigrant students will face negative economic consequences if they do not learn English quickly, classroom teachers may push those students to give up their native language entirely. This push may not only cause self-esteem problems, but it may also have negative consequences for academic achievement (Cummins, 1993).

Two final examples from students' research drive home the interconnections among cultural conflict, the complexities of language use, and the explosive issue of immigration. Myung is a first-grade student, newly arrived in this country. At the time of the interview, she was seated at the back of the class next to a white teacher's aide, who was assisting her in learning English: "It was hard for me to understand what he was teaching me and I couldn't learn anything from him. I felt so alone being separated from the other kids. I felt so different, like I didn't belong there" (Chiu, Tron, & Chou, 1995, p. 10).

Jaime, a bilingual Filipino student-teacher, also expressed anxiety to the researchers:

> When I first came to the United States, I didn't want to speak English even if I knew it. I was scared that the other kids would laugh at me because somebody told me that I had an accent. So I kept quiet all the time even when the teacher called on me and then she thought that I was stupid or something. (Chiu, Tron, & Chou, 1995, p. 12)

We will notice similar patterns of discrimination among other immigrant groups in the examples to follow. The key point here, however, is that through a collaborative relationship with community-based agencies, these teacher-researchers were able to take the lead in acquiring information that, in my judgment, is crucial toward understanding how discrimination works in the classroom. In subsequent chapters, I show how this knowledge of immigrants and language minority students can be coupled with resources in the community to empower teachers and others to take collaborative action. When individuals act together they join the fight to end discrimination and institutional racism in schools. The next example of action research concerns Latino students.

Reaching Out to Latino Parents

Do Latino Parents Want to Be Involved?

A common perception among academic researchers and teachers alike is that low parental involvement adversely contributes to Latino student achievement. Although researchers have identified varying (and conflicting) causes of "low parental involvement" (Arias, 1986; Matute-Bianchi & Eugenia, 1986; Trueba & Delgado-Gaitan, 1991), a widely held explanation is that the values of parents conflict with the values of the school. It is also a fact that low academic achievement among Latino students results, in large part, from the inability of their parents to assist in the learning process.

I do not intend to debate the empirical validity of researchers' claims. Rather, my intention is to explore the implications of the values thesis and its effects on the predominantly middle-class teachers and administrators in American schools. At best, school leaders view the problem of parental involvement among Latino parents as a challenge. At worst, low *parental* expectations for the schools might translate to equally low, and potentially devastating, *teacher* expectations for students.

Stereotypes about parents of minority students are inseparable from typical beliefs about their culture. Another teacher-researcher enrolled in the Crosscultural Language and Academic Development (CLAD) program at UCI put this issue clearly:

> In a study of Boston public schools, interviews with teachers revealed that most teachers defined Latino students' achievement problems in terms of their lack of conceptual understanding in English, lack of motivation, lack of enthusiasm for learning, boredom, and to the difficulties associated with children not retaining what they learned. . . . (Rivera & Nieto, 1993, cited in Spencer, 1995, p. 2)
>
> During my student-teaching I personally encountered these stereotypes of Latino students in the teachers' lounges on several occasions. . . . If damaging messages about Latinos are perpetuated in schools, this might affect how Latino students feel about themselves, their future, and their intelligences which could affect their behavior in a way that Latino students are not motivated to learn and *that they do not value education.* . . . (Spencer, 1995, p. 2, emphasis added)

Pio Pico: An Extraordinary School Community

Mary Spencer, the teacher-researcher quoted above, conducted classroom observations and student interviews at Pio Pico Elementary School in Santa Ana, California. Pio Pico achieved notoriety in the summer of 1995 when, along with the Boys' and Girls' Club of Santa Ana (a national not-for-profit organization that works with at-risk youth), it cohosted a national announcement by President Clinton and the Taco Bell Corporation. The announcement detailed plans by Taco Bell to expand its financial support of the Boys' and Girls' Club to implement gang-prevention programs in schools and local communities.

The school is known for being situated in one of the most densely populated neighborhoods in the country. Despite the massive social problems that result from the social isolation of inner-city residents (Garvin, 1994; Lemann, 1991), the researcher noted that "due to the efforts of the principal, Judy Magsaysay, many of the parents at Pio Pico are directly involved in the school through the PTA, parent ESL classes, the Parent Institute for Quality Education, and parent leadership teams" (Spencer, 1995, p. 3). I can also vouch for this observation. When I accompanied Dr. Suzi Charlton on a field visit to the school and the club, scores of parents were waiting outside to meet with teachers, help escort children home, and participate in the parent activities described above.

The school employs what is known as a *transitional bilingual education model* (Garcia, 1994). Here, native Spanish-speaking elementary age children study academic subjects in their native language until such time as they have mastered English and the content areas. This transition usually takes place between the third and sixth grades in most programs of this type.[4] The school has received numerous grants, both governmental and private. For example, it has used a grant from the State of California to restructure its curriculum around a constructivist model that supports a "thinking, meaning-centered" curriculum (California Department of Education, 1992). Thus, "the school has made extraordinary efforts to increase the academic achievement of [Latino] students and to dramatically increase parent involvement in the school" (Spencer, 1995, p. 4).

Spencer also documented how Latino students at Pio Pico struggle to overcome stereotyping and to excel academically. The following exchange illustrates the very real peer and family pressures that potentially can undermine students' achievement:

Irma: My brother is in high school and he says the boys are not good. But he says he likes school. They [the students at my brother's school] want to be in gangs sometime.

Juan Carlos: I know my cousin says that his friends don't really care about school. They just want to hang out. He says school is really hard and it goes fast.

Maggie: Sometimes my brother says he has some friends [who] tell him that it's not good to study, because when they grow up they can't be who they want to be, and then my brother says that they are not friends. (Spencer, 1995, p. 10)

These conflicts stand in stark contrast to the confidence and enthusiasm that some of the students at Pio Pico School displayed when interviewed by the teacher-researchers.

Javier: I think school is important because we learn a lot of things. We learn about the past. You learn to read things and you learn to control yourself. That way you can get better jobs.

Maggie: It's important to learn because when you grow up you could be . . . a teacher, a doctor, and lots of things.

Some students indicated a preference for math and science. These students, whose parents and college role models have encouraged them to excel in disciplines often proving difficult for minorities, even spoke of attending college.

Regige: I want to go to UCI. I want to study math and science.

Anna: I want to study music in college.

Rolando: I like studying math. [It's a] challenge, and I want to go to college to be a teacher.

Maggie: Yes, I expect to go to college. I want to learn psychology, geography, and I want to be a teacher. (Spencer, 1995, p. 5)

In conclusion, this chapter has illustrated the power of teacher-led research to produce knowledge of school community and neighborhood life. Although the examples are drawn from teacher-preparation programs, it seems reasonable that a climate for the everyday practice of action research and inquiry—leading to the identification of and alternate resolutions for genuine problems in the school—could be established. A collaborative model of action research could also be of service to local communities whose students are experiencing discrimination, both at home and in their neighborhoods.

Notes

1. The term *action research* is greatly overused and, at times, controversial, particularly within the academic community, which tends to be skeptical about its validity. However, when aimed at problem solving in the schools as well as the testing of ideas and strategies, and when making no scientific claims, action research is potentially a very empowering tool for classroom teachers. Anderson, Herr, & Nihlen (1994) define the term as follows: "Practitioner [action] research is done within an action-oriented setting in which reflection on action is the driving force of the research. This tension inherent in combining action and research is captured in the term traditionally used to describe this type of inquiry: 'action research.' " (p. xxi).

2. Authors Grace Chiu, Thuy-Linh Tron, and David Chou entitled their research paper "Beyond Whiz Kids: The Illusion Behind Asian Stereotypes." Summer Bilingual Cultural Language and Academic Development Institute, University of California, Irvine, 1995.

3. In 1995, this conflict was vividly illustrated in Southern California when an Asian American high school valedictorian committed suicide, purportedly as a result of the cross-pressures he faced about his personal identity.

4. Bilingual programs are a source of intense ideological conflict. I note that federal law and state education policy require that English (in the form of ESL classes) be included in any bilingual education program. The overwhelming majority of these programs are of the "transitional" type; the often-unstated goal is quick assimilation into mainstream American language (English) and culture. A contrasting, and much less popular, model is known as "maintenance" bilingual education, where students often receive continual instruction in their native language in the hope that some will retain their language and culture throughout high school.

5

Deepening
Student Governance

In this chapter, I call for what is perhaps the most controversial of measures to help alleviate discrimination in public schools—student governance. By *governance* I mean both formal and informal participation by students in forming school policy, such as curriculum choices, classroom management, and decisions about discipline. Although I generally limit my proposal primarily to middle- and secondary-school students, I am a reform advocate who falls into Maxcy's (1995a, 1995b) "democratic maximizers" category. I believe that given appropriate classroom activities, student identity at all levels of instruction can mature into full subjectivity (Biesta, 1994). To strengthen this call, I will cite examples from public schools, mainly drawing from the case studies in Apple and Beane's book, *Democratic Schools* (1995).

Recognizing the Power of Student Voice

My argument is that students suffer discrimination in schools mostly as a result of their lack of voice (Weis & Fine, 1993). In both types of discrimination—identity and academic—it is easy to see how these two concepts are linked in practice. Identity discrimination—the expectation that students who "look different" are at risk of dropping out of school or, worse, of joining gangs—often springs

51

from students' not having a say in school policy. Dress codes, however innocuous, tend to work against students who resist the hidden curriculum of the school. For example, at Neighborhood High, African American students, who had difficulty separating student culture from neighborhood and home cultures (see Mirón & Lauria, 1995; Murry, Bogotch, & Mirón, 1995), complained that some white teachers often mistook them for criminals. Similarly, students at Neighborhood High who were tracked in general or vocational classes expressed amazement that Vietnamese ESL students apparently moved on to graduate with honors. Students from other racial minority groups viewed the Vietnamese students' achievements with skepticism because many Vietnamese students had begun in lower-level academic tracks as the school's way of addressing language difficulties. Both forms of discrimination, as I will show below, could be resolved with student governance mechanisms and policies.

The Question of Maturity

Educators have often asserted that young people are not mature enough to participate in school decisions. To be sure, many are not. However, if we as a society value our democratic heritage and way of life, then what better place to gain these skills and practice this participation than in public schools?

The question usually posed is "At what age can students begin?" Often overlooked, however, are the social-class biases inherent in the issue of age. Upper-middle-class families, for instance, value questioning from their children about family decisions. Anyon's (1980) research has shown, moreover, that schools located in upper-middle-class neighborhoods encourage active, hands-on learning and students' construction of their own knowledge. Although Anyon's study of fifth-grade students (see also Anyon, 1994) does not explicitly concern student participation in school governance, her empirical work has strong implications for the model I propose here.

First, it is clear from observing upper-middle-class families that students can begin the governance process fairly early on. In addition, models of learning such as the Association for Supervision and Curriculum Development's (ASCD) "constructivism" (Brooks &

Brooks, 1993) assume that students benefit when they are copartici-
pants in teaching and learning. Second, instructional practices in
working-class, neighborhood-based public schools often function to
control student behavior, rather than provide opportunities for
deeper learning (Mirón, 1996). Third, and perhaps most consequen-
tially, the forms of the curriculum—high or low content, relevance to
learners' needs, standardized versus community-specific, etc. (Olsen, 1994)—as well as the types of pedagogical activities contribute
to social and cultural reproduction that may hinder the socioeconomic mobility of large numbers of students. Thus teachers may be
incorrect in their beliefs about which student governance models are
developmentally appropriate insofar as matters of curriculum and
learning are concerned. The issue is of very practical concern and
much more than a philosophical debate between theorists.

Responding to a Double Message

I need to be clear about what I mean exactly by student governance. The meaning extends beyond formal participation in school
policy making (for example, Associated Student Body and Student
Council). Following the precepts of postmodernism (Beyer & Liston,
1992; Mirón, 1996), student governance embraces the idea that multiple voices—including those of students as well as the collaboration
of teachers and students—will characterize much of the daily activity in the classroom. Specifically, students are empowered to help
decide what knowledge is potentially relevant for their academic *and*
personal goals and are able to act on their choices about curriculum
relevance. My research (Mirón, 1996) shows that school culture
largely influences the quality and intensity of much student resistance to the formal and hidden curriculum. At Neighborhood High,
for instance, students complained that academic work was equivalent to busywork. Conversely, at City High students experienced a
direct connection between what they learned (for example, writing
and social studies) and their future goals. Although African American students at City High did not have a formal mechanism to address their academic concerns, the overall tradition of instructional
excellence at this magnet school virtually guaranteed the support of
their career goals.

Gaining Experience Through Involvement

It is not enough, however, simply to give voice to student needs. If students are to become effective participants in our democratic society— that is, informed and active citizens in their local communities—then they need direct experience that active involvement makes a difference in their day-to-day lives. They must be given a vehicle to test the consequences of their actions.

Biesta (1994) calls this school practice the development of *practical intersubjectivity*. He argues that from both a philosophical and a practical point of view, the fundamental problem in education is its "asymmetry." Students are responsible for their own academic achievement—just like full-grown adults—yet their voices are not considered where policy matters affecting teaching and learning are concerned.

In the final analysis, Biesta's complex theoretical argument is relatively simple to understand: either students (middle school and beyond) are treated like adults or they are treated like children. They cannot be both. It is potentially devastating for at-risk students in the inner city and in poor rural areas to be treated like adults (with matters of achievement left up to them), on the one hand, yet denied the "person right" (Apple, 1988) to take action upon the curriculum, on the other hand. Such a pedagogical double bind exacerbates the academic and social inequalities ethnic minority students already experience. Furthermore, it virtually denies them any meaningful opportunity to engage in measures that might alleviate the cultural and racial barriers to learning (see Spindler & Spindler, 1994).

In summary, there are developmental as well as pedagogical reasons to justify active student participation in school governance. If we are serious about a just and equitable society that is free of discrimination and institutional racism in public schools, then we must be serious about making schools—as public institutions—more democratic. In the next section I borrow from Apple and Beane's book *Democratic Schools* (1995) to illustrate concretely how researchers and educational leaders in schools might develop this ideal.

Practicing Democracy in Student Government

Michael Apple and James Beane (1995) provide concrete descriptions of public schools that succeed in the practice of democracy.

They show the dimensions and possibilities of how school "actors" (students, administrators, teachers, and parents) can take deliberate steps to ensure that democratic ideals are achievable. This is similar to my concept of *democracy as an antidote for discrimination and institutional racism.*

My purpose in providing illustrative cases, however, is to analyze how the common goals of educators in and of themselves point to the practical, incremental steps to take. With this knowledge, school leaders may assist minority students in achieving specific benefits: equity, social justice, and academic excellence. Apple and Beane (1995) nicely summarize the lofty goals of the public schools they describe.

> In the midst of widespread attacks on [public] education, we must keep alive the long tradition of democratic school reform that has played such a valuable role in making many schools lively and powerful places for those who go to them. Rather than giving up on the idea of the "public" schools and moving down the path toward privatization, we need to focus on schools that work. Despite some people's relentless attempts to make us think otherwise, we do not have to resign ourselves to choosing between a failing public school system and market initiatives such as voucher plans or for-profit schools run by private firms like the Edison Project or Education Alternatives, Inc. There are public schools throughout this country where the hard work of teachers, administrators, parents, community activists and students has paid off. These are the schools that are alive with excitement, even in sometimes depressing and difficult circumstances. These are the schools in which teachers and students alike are engaged in serious work that results in rich and vital learning experiences for all. (p. 3)

The following cases represent schools where both majority and minority students also appear to respect each other, and where school personnel treat students equally and equitably.

The Case of Central Park East

Deborah Meir, former codirector of Central Park East High School in East Harlem, New York, has become something of a household name in school-reform circles. Her work, along with that of her colleagues and students, has been featured on PBS documentaries and has been the subject of national panels on education reform. She generally talks about taking a school that "nobody wanted" and helping to transform it into a model of a public high school for the nation.

Student government based on core values. Central Park East is part of Theodore Sizer's "Coalition of Essential Schools." As a member of this national network, the school, under Meir's leadership, embraces the following core values:

- *Less is more.* Students should become experts in at least one field of knowledge.
- *Personalization.* Teaching and learning serve the needs of individual students. For example, the maximum total number of students that any single teacher sees in one school day is 80.
- *Goal setting.* Teachers and administrators, as well as fellow students, set high academic standards. Students demonstrate mastery of academic content through portfolios and other performative measures.
- *Student as worker.* The teacher's role is that of a "coach." Teachers encourage students to, in effect, teach themselves. Thus, students discover answers and solutions and learn by doing rather than by simply repeating what textbooks (or teachers) say. (Apple & Beane, 1995, p. 27)

I would like to underscore the significance of the last principle. As I have mentioned in my study of student resistance, students from Neighborhood High greatly resented the irrelevance of learning that accompanied continuous control over academic work. Many of the students we interviewed at Neighborhood High (see Anfara & Mirón, 1996; Lauria, Mirón, & Dashner, 1994) suffered from poor schooling on two fronts: (1) they attended a school where substitute teaching was routine, especially in key areas such as algebra; (2) they experienced school as busywork, largely as a result of teachers' fear of violence. Because many white teachers perceived African American males as hoodlums or potential gang members, they exercised control over student behavior by filling up class time with ditto

sheets and exercises from the text, and also prevented social interaction in general within the classroom. The administration also
maintained a policy of shutting down schoolwide assemblies because of a similar fear of school violence. The idea of having students
assume responsibility for their own learning (treating them like
adults) would go a long way toward eliminating such negative practices on the part of teachers and students. Perhaps administrators at
schools such as Neighborhood High might even see their way clear
to restoring student assemblies and other forms of cultural activity
that would nurture a sense of pride.

Meir and Schwartz (1995) detail the organizational structure of
Central Park East "in which people—students and students, students and teachers, and teachers and teachers, and their families—
could think aloud together and jointly make decisions" (pp. 29-35).
In other words, the structure of the school furthered the principles of
the "Coalition of Essential Schools" and the ideals of participatory
democracy. Moreover, the school moved beyond theoretically de-
rived, utopian democratic beliefs (see Giroux, 1991) and instead defined for itself what this practice meant on a daily basis.

Meir and Schwartz (1995) attributed the success of the school to
certain student qualities, each of which teachers and administrators
were committed to help cultivate and model. Two specific qualities
are empathy and skepticism.[1] *Empathy* refers to "the ability to see a
situation from the eyes of another, and *skepticism* is the tendency to
wonder about the validity of what we [as a school community have]
encountered" (p. 30).

Success determined by outcome goals. Academically, the school
leadership from Central Park East instilled democratic principles by
closely examining and describing the expected *outcomes*, not solely
in terms of achievement on test scores (although the authors report that
90% of the graduates attend college), but also in practical terms of what
a thoughtful person might be like after receiving such an education.
"Thoughtfulness" consists of addressing these five questions: (1)
How do you know what you know? (providing evidence), (2) From
whose perspective is knowledge and evidence presented?, (3) How
is this event or your work connected to others?, (4) What if things
were not as they are now? (supposition, imagination), and (5) Why
is this (work) important? By deliberately organizing classroom

activities around the fundamental goal of nurturing the development of a thoughtful, skeptical, and empathetic person, teacher-leaders enable students to exercise participatory democracy in the area
of most importance: making decisions about the classroom—that is,
about teaching, the curriculum, and learning. In this way students
are provided the "agency" (see Giddens, 1986) to affect classroom
life, without which democratic schooling becomes largely irrelevant
to students.

How do these philosophical principles and operational procedures give life to the values of equity, social justice, and excellence
that have been denied students who have historically experienced
discrimination in schools and classrooms? On a social level, being
empathetic means respecting (and, therefore, valuing) the life experiences of others. All students can thus learn to respect and value
differences, the hallmark of antidiscriminatory practices. On a psychological level, minority students can learn to gain perspective and
realize that many of the racial injustices they have suffered stem
from "systemic" factors, even though institutional racism is often
also a matter of individual attitudes and actions. By developing the
"habits of mind, work, and heart" (Apple & Beane, 1995, p. 27), students can begin to empower themselves and feel less victimized.

Conducting a graduation examination. It is a tradition of Central
Park East to establish an examination committee for all graduating
seniors. This committee is responsible for assessing whether or not
students have acquired the "five habits of mind" that are outcome
goals for every student. Each student's advisor appoints the members
of the committee, with the exception that a student may choose one
adult (for example, a parent) to serve on the graduation committee.

Meir and Schwartz (1995) detailed the first meeting of one student's graduation committee. The student, Monique, chose to present a paper on the subject of AIDS. Monique was prepared to address questions about the sources of her research into AIDS; fellow
students who had been through the committee process warned her
that such questions come up frequently. However, the drift of the
questions changed dramatically, moving from questions about the
credibility of information to real-life situations that tested judgment
and strength of character as well. Meir, the former principal, noted:

[T]he questions quickly become less predictable. 'Monique,' I ask, 'you spoke of doctors who screened patients for the HIV virus without their knowledge or permission. You see this as a bad thing, an invasion of their privacy. Just last Sunday I saw a TV program about Cuba and their response to the AIDS epidemic. In Cuba they test everyone. They don't ask permission. When they find an HIV-positive person, they quarantine them. They are put in a comfortable place with good food and excellent health care, but they must stay there. Period. One result is that they have generally lessened the spread of the disease. What if they were to do that here?' (Meir & Schwartz, 1995, p. 33)

It is obvious from the case study of Central Park East that participatory democracy in public schools is directly linked to student-centered learning. Students at this school are able to see the concrete results of their participation in classroom decisions—their active "voice," broadly conceived—by the fact that their mastery of content *empowers them to be in control of much of the agenda of learning.* Moreover, in addition to the fact that students here have a substantive voice in curriculum decisions that affect the classroom, by being able to choose an adult member for their graduation committee—moreover, a member other than a teacher—they also have some say in decisions that affect the entire school. In Monique's case, this choice reflected on the credibility of the entire school as measured by the quality of its graduates. I suggest that democracy is not an end in itself in this case. It is a viable tool to pass on the experience of empowerment.

The latter point is vividly illustrated in a second example, again taken from Apple and Beane (1995). The school is La Escuela Fratney, an elementary two-way bilingual school situated in inner-city Milwaukee, Wisconsin.

Collaborating for an Antiracist Curriculum

The Case of La Escuela Fratney

The power of language. La Escuela Fratney, a school governed jointly by parents and teachers, is rather remarkable in its delivery of a full, two-way bilingual program.[2] The school serves 360 students, from 4-year-olds in kindergarten to fifth graders, and has a population that is 65% Latino, 20% African American, 13% white, and 2% Asian American and Native American. Approximately 70% of the students are eligible for free lunches, not atypical for inner-city schools serving large percentages of low-income students (see Mirón & St. John, 1994).

The bilingual education program at La Escuela Fratney is part and parcel of the larger efforts of the school faculty and administration to eliminate institutional racism by having direct conversations about the role of power, race, gender, and ethnicity in our society. Many educators consider this dialogue to be a mandatory step toward eliminating discrimination in the classroom because school restructuring activities are tied to the attempt to acknowledge—and do something about—unequal power relations (Sarason, 1990).

The classroom is organized around "dominant" and "subordinate" language groups, with native speakers of English and Spanish in the same classroom. Instruction is conducted 50% in each language. This model "avoids separating children by language dominance and gives meaning and purpose to the acquisition of two languages." Teachers follow a "strict separation of the two languages and language environments," which forces children to use the second language yet encourages teachers to be consistent about conducting instruction in the target language (Peterson, 1995, p. 65).

Like the high school students at Central Park East, elementary students here are provided intense experiences where they participate in classroom decisions. For example, when the faculty discovered at the end of the second year that English was still too dominant, teachers formed a committee that included kindergarten students and their parents to advise the faculty on what to do. Kindergartners! Their input led to a decision to adopt a schoolwide method of instruction in their kindergarten bilingual classes wherein students would rotate, receiving Spanish and English instruction in alternate rooms.

Resolving ethnic conflict. The leaders of La Escuela Fratney—teachers, parents, students, and administrators—have tackled the thorny issue of institutional racism at their school and in society. Among white middle-class parents, the expected complaints about having to stress "minority" history and denying their children the right to their European heritage have led to some stormy meetings.

Ethnic conflict between white and Puerto Rican parents ensued when the white parents questioned the practice of excluding the pledge of allegiance, and a Puerto Rican parent roared in retort "how angry she became every time she had to recite the pledge of allegiance, because it reminded her that Puerto Rico has endured decades of U.S. colonial rule without 'liberty and justice for all' " (Peterson, 1995, p. 66).

Peterson makes a significant point that I reemphasize in my analysis here; that is, "such differences of opinion don't go away" (p. 67). All too often, school personnel want to sweep the controversy engendered by multicultural education under the rug. They feign resolution and move on to the next point. As I argued in Chapter 3, this practice is wrong. First, it denies the "teachable moment" in which to acknowledge our differences. Second, it sends the wrong signal to students in the classroom that discussion about value conflicts is taboo. In the case of the white and Puerto Rican parents, the full airing of their conflict led to positive, affirmative steps toward fulfillment of the antiracist goals of the school.

La Escuela Fratney implemented a yearlong process wherein parents and faculty collaborated on hammering out what an antiracist, multicultural education would mean on an everyday basis. Eventually, this process, in concert with more traditional discussions among the site-based council, the parent curriculum committee,[3] and the staff, resulted in five written drafts that produced a joint parent-teacher statement that "outlined the philosophy and implementation of multicultural, antiracist education" at the school (Peterson, 1995, p. 68).

Benefiting from peer discipline. La Escuela Fratney affords students the opportunity to influence schoolwide decisions. Through its "cooperative learning and discipline" approach, students are empowered to assume beliefs and the responsibility to act upon them (Finnan, St. John, McCarthy, & Slovacek, 1996). This is a phenomenal opportunity for elementary students.

Peterson (1995) freely and candidly admitted that establishing this practice was not easy.

Cooperative learning and classroom management come up in almost any discussion of democracy in schools. The first year of the Fratney program verged on disaster because we overestimated the responsibilities our students would be able to handle. Specifically, we failed to anticipate that a large percentage of the children who chose to come to our school were having little success at their previous school. Many students lacked basic self-management skills. They were unable to handle rights as simple as being able to take a pass and go to the bathroom on their own (without teacher permission). We realized that we had to consciously help students make the transition from the past, *where they had been treated like sheep, to the future, where we wanted them to act like responsible human beings.* (p. 70, emphasis added)

This passage highlights the endemic conflicts that a school community must endure if it is to move from a hierarchical, top-down model of educational governance to one focusing on students' rights and responsibilities. Such conflicts can be successfully negotiated. However, many schools are unable to accomplish this feat, due largely to the refusal of the administration to let go of control (see Mirón & St. John, 1994).

What did the leaders in the school community do? They obtained Chapter I funding to hire a full-time self-esteem specialist. This specialist did more than administer a program, however. She was in the classroom, team teaching with the regular classroom teachers, and focusing on developing specific intervention techniques to foster self-esteem in children. The school also implemented a "cross-age" tutoring program as well as a peer mediation model to handle discipline issues.

These techniques, which vividly illustrate the type of student governance I advocate, embody a broader strategy that Peterson (1995, p. 70) terms "cooperative management." Similar to the method used to create school "charters," described in Michelle Fine's *Chartering Urban School Reform* (a case study of the Philadelphia School Collaborative, 1994), cooperative management encourages teachers to divide their classrooms into small groups. Each group typically has six students and its own set of books and bookshelf. The groups elect their own captain, who assumes responsibility for ensuring that books and other materials are in order and that students are paying attention and engaged in classroom activities.

This technique illustrates what Biesta (1994) calls the development of "practical intersubjectivity." As I discussed earlier, this philosophical term means that out of practical social interaction stems students' sense of identity and their position as participating students, and, potentially, as citizens in a democracy. What is important about such techniques is that power, defined as control over student behavior, is delegated from teacher to student. In other words, traditional power relations are deliberately rearranged in the classroom and throughout the school. Thus students who experience discrimination have a voice—and a means—to empower themselves. The fact that they rely on themselves, as students with "adult-like" rights and responsibilities, means that *no one individual—teacher, student, or principal*—has control over students' lives. Discrimination, defined as relationships of injustice and inequity, simply cannot be reproduced in a context prohibiting unilateral exercise of power by school personnel. It is therefore up to students, through the acquisition of psychological self-esteem and practical intersubjectivity, to exercise greater control over their own destiny.

To conclude, I maintain that resisting discrimination is largely about the awareness of who has control in the classroom and in the school. The two types of discrimination identified in this book—identity and academic—result from a perceived powerlessness by students (see Everhart, 1983; Willis, 1977). I have shown elsewhere (Lauria, Mirón, & Dashner, 1994; Mirón, 1996) what happens when students exercise power, specifically over their right to a quality public education.

The key to overcoming discrimination is in restoring students' sense of their own efficacy in the classroom and their capacity to exercise power in the whole school, and, indeed, in the wider society. By restructuring schools along the lines of the case studies presented in this chapter—that is, by deliberately altering unequal power relations, tilting them in favor of students and their parents—students can become human agents, fully capable themselves of overcoming discrimination and racism in schools and in their personal lives. They need not depend on adults or formal policies if simply provided the formal and informal organizational structures to act with the confidence and authority afforded mature adults (Anfara & Mirón, 1996).

Notes

1. Interestingly, these qualities mirror scholarly work about school re-structuring. For example, skepticism embodies the spirit of Maxcy's (1995a) "critical-pragmatic" approach in his book *Democracy, Chaos, and the New School Order*. Similarly, empathy is compatible with the ethic of care as the basis for school change and new administrative-leadership practices. For the latter, see Nel Noddings (1992), *The Challenge to Care in Schools*, and Lynn Beck (1994), *Reclaiming Educational Administration as a Caring Profession*.

2. Much empirical research on bilingual education over the past 2 dec-ades has established that two-way bilingual programs, where equal atten-tion is paid to native and second language instruction, is the exception. Ideo-logically, given the "English Only" movements in California, Florida, and other states, and in light of the politics of the new nativism, it is difficult for educators to garner public support for this form of bilingual education.

3. The school is governed by committees consisting of almost equal numbers of teachers and parents.

Forging Community Partnerships

In the previous chapter, I suggested that ultimately it is the student who must overcome discrimination. However, students need not act alone in attaining their goal. As I will establish in this chapter, schools and the nonprofit sector also have important roles to play. School leaders must create new organizational structures (similar to those found at La Escuela Fratney, described in Chapter 5) that facilitate students' awareness of their own capacity for agency, the power to act upon circumstances (Giddens, 1986; Starratt, 1991, 1994).

This chapter illustrates how to build bridges with a potentially powerful ally of public schools—community-based nonprofit organizations (Heath & McLaughlin, 1993). My research as a participant-observer working with nonprofits and public schools (Bogotch, Mirón & Garvin, 1993; Mirón, 1995; Mirón & Wimpelberg, 1989) has shown that there is tremendous potential for school leaders, especially classroom teachers, to engage the support of nonprofit organizations to further both the academic and social purposes of schools (Spring, 1985). Although problems may arise when schools enter into collaborative ventures with "outside" organizations whose goals may differ (Mirón, 1988), the potential for gain far outweighs any possible losses. Such gains might include anything from the furnishing of basic classroom supplies to the saving from extinction a school of choice.[1]

I present here two case studies of schools that have received extraordinary benefits from nonprofit support organizations, the Friends of the New Orleans Center for Creative Arts (FON) and the Boys' and Girls' Club of Santa Ana, California. These nonprofit organizations helped shape the educational environment of two public schools, the New Orleans Center for Creative Arts (NOCCA) and Pio Pico Elementary School.

A Partnership for Equality:
Friends of NOCCA

Founded in 1982, Friends of the New Orleans Center for Creative Arts (FON) have as their mission to provide a margin of excellence and support for professional arts training at the New Orleans Center for Creative Arts, a nationally acclaimed arts training center serving metropolitan New Orleans. During the past 5 years, FON has undertaken the enormous task of financing a new $21 million facility located in a socioeconomically changing, historic New Orleans neighborhood.

At first glance, this task is quite impressive. On further reflection, it appears extraordinary that a small nonprofit organization with a 35-member board of directors could find the fiscal and political wherewithal to secure more than $16 million in state capital outlay[2] funds; $5 million in support from individuals, corporations, and foundations; and enough community support to encourage the Orleans Parish School Board and its new superintendent, Dr. Morris Holmes, to authorize the construction of a new school. Furthermore, given the current backlash against government funding for the arts and humanities characteristic of members of the "Gingrich Revolution," the case of FON's success provides dedicated public school personnel with strong reason to hope. For our purposes, the emphasis of the board of directors on making *equal access to quality public education* a meaningful social reality is a powerful example of how academic excellence need not be a model for exclusion. Indeed, by emphasizing the innate cultural diversity of the performing arts, while maintaining rigorous academic standards, students learn to appreciate the sense of their own cultural identities.

An Unfunded Priority: Relocation of the Arts School

The New Orleans public schools are similar to schools in other large urban school districts—they have dire financial needs. In particular, the many decayed school buildings, the large number of non-air-conditioned classrooms, and the overall lack of basic pupil supplies make it difficult for teachers to attend to routine instruction. Schools such as Carver High have drawn the attention of national education writers, including Gene Maeroff (1988), because of their deplorable conditions. In 1995, school district planners estimated that it would cost nearly half a billion dollars to bring the school district up to minimum facility standards.

Understandably, the Orleans Parish School Board, despite its general support of the mission of NOCCA, chose not to fund the construction of a new arts school. The center remained on its long list of "unfunded priorities." The first task of the board of directors and administrative leadership of FON was to seek consensus to change the budgetary status of the school. This meant raising the visibility of the high school to a level where the school board would desire to build a new facility. Simply finding the funds to construct the school would not necessarily change the minds of the majority African American school board members (whose constituents from their political districts needed new schools of their own) to the point where the arts school would become a *fundable priority*. Neither the funding prospects nor the political situation was favorable.

Racial Politics: Interaction With the School Board

The issue of race crept up quietly but repeatedly in the debates about the fate of the proposed new facility. NOCCA was located in a white upper-middle-class neighborhood in the "Uptown" section of New Orleans. Although the school itself maintained a 50% black, 50% white student body, most of the members of the FON Board of Directors were white. Despite the commitment of its outstanding faculty to racial equality and to high expectations for all of its students, the school, as well as FON, had acquired a reputation for elitism.[3] The FON Board of Directors fought a battle for the school on two fronts: internally within the district bureaucracy and externally within the majority African American school board, which served a constituency that believed the center's students could afford private tuition and therefore were taking advantage of the school district.

FON was convinced that the Orleans Parish School Board could survive these complex political overtones if the school could be built without any district funds—and if the school were relocated to an area that was accessible to more of its low-income and minority students living at a distance from the old Uptown school. It established a racially and socially broad-based committee (the NOCCA/ Riverfront Task Force) to oversee the relocation of the school to a neighborhood situated adjacent to the Mississippi River and convenient to district bus routes and public transportation. This neighborhood, Faubourg-Marigny, had experienced economic decline and is now characterized by low- to middle-income families. The relocation of the school came to be perceived as part of a larger strategy of neighborhood revitalization that might be stimulated by a premier arts high school, open in the evenings for community functions.

Securing Districtwide Endorsement

On November 22, 1993, FON appeared at a meeting of the Orleans Parish School Board to present a status report. It brought a commitment of $16 million in state capital outlay funds and a "cooperative endeavor agreement" written by several state agencies, FON's Board of Directors, and the school board to execute a public-private partnership to relocate the school to the Faubourg-Marigny area. Minutes from that meeting reveal the complexity of the project, including a glimpse into how a small nonprofit organization, dedicated to improving education and professional training in the performing arts, worked collaboratively with a school district to overcome substantial racial and political baggage. But the minutes can never reveal the behind-the-scenes story caused by the delicate problems of new relationships.

Although the subject of race was to come to the forefront in subsequent meetings, when school board members explicitly demanded higher black enrollment, *the FON collaborative process remained racially and politically inclusive*. A number of individuals stepped forward to support the endeavor. And, as it happened, many of the most vocal supporters were African American. The board of directors also needed approval and support from city hall and black mayors Sidney Barthelemy and, later, Marc Morial. Of great help was that at the time of the presentation to the Orleans Parish School Board, the president of FON was an African American who was a longtime friend of many school board members and who took the leadership to win support from the school board. Furthermore, one of the members of the task force, Gail Glapion, was an African American who served as school board president during the crucial stages of gaining endorsement, both from the school board and from its newly hired superintendent, Dr. Morris Holmes.

Although the potential existed for racial issues to dominate decisions pertaining to the relocation of the school, the positive, collaborative actions of school board members, district facility planners, and the Office of the Mayor, *regardless of race*, resulted in a win-win situation. Any negative racial politics became of background concern to the shared vision of providing greater opportunities for public school students to benefit from a world-class professional arts program. As I will establish below, the substantive focus on the arts—as a racial-ethnic cultural bridge—is an ideal vehicle to further the equity and equality goals of *collaboration as a process value*.

Acquiring a site. The Norfolk Southern Railroad Company owned the proposed site for the new school. The FON Board of Directors acquired this property through a gift from Norfolk Southern and a complex financing package from a consortium of New Orleans banks. FON did not ask the school board to contribute money toward the purchase of the property; however, as part of its "cooperative endeavor agreement" with the nonprofit organization and the state, which guaranteed construction in the form of secured bonds, the district committed to the facility maintenance and the delivery of the instructional program a commitment approximating the $800,000 per year current annual budget for NOCCA.

Minding the store. FON played an incredible leadership role in securing state and private funds to acquire a site and begin construction of a new school. But the group went beyond assuming an external role. It also supported the principal in his efforts to satisfy central administration, particularly the associate superintendent and superintendent of schools.

During the peak activity of FON's negotiatioms to acquire the site, the school board hired Dr. Morris Holmes as superintendent. Holmes was relentless in his goal of improving reading achievement and other quantitative measures of student performance. He accomplished this by requiring all schools, including "special purpose schools" like NOCCA, to comply with his new vision of the school district: "working together to build respect for life, property and learning."

Superintendent Holmes subscribed to six *simple measures of success* including parental involvement, safe schools, monitoring of instruction, reading achievement, learning readiness, and, most significantly, effective community partnerships. At every meeting called by the area superintendent to monitor the results in meeting these indicators for the performing arts school, the principal invited the FON Executive Director, and occasionally the president of its board of directors. As an active member of the black community and a former public school teacher, the president was prominent in the community and a known friend of the school district.

The administrative situation was such that the principal and the center's teaching staff of professional artists needed to be unusually sensitive to the pressures inside the district to centralize curriculum planning and outcomes. At times, this was very frustrating to the staff of the school. As an advisor to the school and as a researcher employing participation-observation methods (see Anderson, Herr, & Nihlen, 1994, esp. pp. 130-133), I remember facilitating a teaching staff discussion of ways to emphasize NOCCA's high academic standards in a manner that would avoid the appearance of elitism. Simultaneously, I encouraged the school to capitalize on its enormous community support (in addition to FON, it had a strong parent support group) and to seek to track success in line with its special academic mission "to prepare all students to take the next logical step immediately upon graduation, while, at the same time, allowing them to enhance their nonarts options."

The unique role of the school as a training site for professional arts—including dance, music, theater, visual arts, and creative writing—may have enhanced its image as an "elitist Uptown school." Protected by the principal, teachers, and parents, and embodied in the work of FON in building a world-class facility, the ideals of the school served to shield it from an inert bureaucracy or, worse, entanglement in racial issues. Had the school not fostered such strong community ties from its inception, it is unlikely that a new building would be under construction today. The role of the arts is of sufficient vitality that it may be the most promising bridge between cultures. Judging from the New Orleans story, education through the arts can be a powerful key to the elimination of discrimination and institutional racism in public schools.

Resisting Gang Identification:
The Boys' and Girls' Club

Of course, the arts are not the only vehicle for bridging cultural chasms. Also of importance is the effort to build support systems that lead to more self-esteem for public school children—afterschool programs, positive parenting classes, and opportunities for academic success. In this regard, the Boys' and Girls' Club, a national nonprofit organization, has become a model institution across the country.

An Influential After-School Program at Pio Pico School

Identity and residence. The Boys' and Girls' Club of Santa Ana, California, serves 3,000 children. Approximately 88% of the population is Latino. Yet in the neighborhood surrounding Pio Pico Elementary School, 98% of the population is Latino. According to demographic data provided by the Club staff, 26,000 children reside within a one-mile radius of the school. It is the second most densely populated area in the United States.[4]

A growing body of scholarly literature (Bourgeois, 1995; Haymes, 1995; Keith & Pile, 1993; Mirón & Lauria, 1995; Soja, 1990) suggests that there exist strong interrelationships between identity and residence. Furthermore, the culture of a school plays an intermediary role in the formation of ethnic identity (see Chapter 1). The location of the club directly across the street from Pio Pico School decreases the possibility that students will identify with gangs in the neighborhood. The partnership between the school and the club helps children at risk of gang membership and gang violence redefine who they are and who they can become. Overall, students at Pio Pico see themselves as enrolling in college in the future (see Chapter 3); children in the after-school programs see themselves as learning social and technical skills that may provide a ticket out of poverty—and out of the geographic determinant of poverty, the barrio or ghetto.

Confronting gang violence. Deservedly or not, Santa Ana, a city in Orange County with a population of approximately 300,000, has acquired a reputation for gang violence. In 1995, for example, the city reported more than 40 deaths related to gangs. City leaders complain that businesses such as the South Coast Plaza Mall, one of the county's most prestigious shopping venues, are biased against the city. For example, a number of Santa Ana firms claim to reside in Costa Mesa, an adjacent, more affluent suburb.

To be associated with a locale of ill repute eventually wears on the adults and children who live there. In particular, the majority Latino residents must vigorously defend their neighborhoods from gang violence. They also struggle against the *social threat* of prejudice fueled by the actions of leaders of commerce who avoid association with the city. At Pio Pico School, Principal Judy Magsaysay has joined forces with the Boys' and Girls' Club to offer a quality after-school program. Children in Grades 1 to 6 are provided enriching educational and social activities, including computer instruction, to help circumvent gang membership in the future.

Such a program requires a delicate balance that is susceptible to potential conflicts. For example, the Club insists on consistent attendance even during holidays, when a number of children go home to be with families in Mexico. Nevertheless, the alternative for many children is to succumb to a life "in the margins" simply because there are no other realistic means to challenge the emotional allure of gang culture.

I believe that what the Boys' and Girls' Club provides is a mainstream outlet for Latino school children, increasingly at risk of being identified as "known gang members." What the club offers are the inexpensive resources (physical and human), as well as the social structure, to support the academic mission of its neighboring school. Put otherwise, the club is the vehicle for society to certify that children are not gang members. Simultaneously, students can say to the world: "I am an individual. Although I may look like a violent youth offender, my association with this institution proves that I am not."

Sports as a key outlet. The club regularly employs high school students who each work 20 hours per week or more supervising after-school activities. Student researchers in the BCLAD program (see Chapter 3) discovered that participation in sports and recreational activities at the club had a very positive effect on Latino students. The high school supervisors experienced a community bond with their elementary-age counterparts, and the students at Pio Pico had a place to go after school.[5]

Fees to families are nominal—$5 per year for the use of the weight room, basketball court, soccer field, and arts and crafts room. There is also a computer lab and a game room. Several high school student employees told researchers that they had made friends while playing soccer after school at the club (Gullingsrud, 1995):

> When asked what his life would be like without the Club, Gilbert responded, "I would be at the streets, wandering around. This keeps me from getting involved in gangs." Azalia said that without the Club's influence she would be a "gangbanger" and a runaway, to get attention. When asked the same question [as Azalia] Ariana replied, "I would be a troublemaker, big time."(p. 9)

It appears that a primary reason for the success of the club in the neighborhood surrounding Pio Pico is its location. It provides a safe place for students to go, as well as employment for high school students in Santa Ana. It also assists administrators who are too often overburdened with social problems largely not of the school's making. They are under perpetual siege for apparent lack of academic achievement and may be tempted to overemphasize the role of academics because of political or cultural pressures.

Nonprofit organizations like the Boys' and Girls' Club offer a powerful human and physical resource—literally, a safe, nurturing place to send school children. Principal Judy Magsaysay recognizes the invaluable resource the club offers Pio Pico. She strives hard for, and achieves, high levels of parental and community support. In doing so, she has redefined the school as a place where caring flourishes (Beck, 1994; Noddings, 1994). By participating in legitimate after-school programs, at-risk children are not at odds with the dominant middle-class culture.

In the sections that follow I show how the partnership between the Boys' and Girls' Club of Santa Ana and Pio Pico Elementary School has expanded to include university researchers and internship experiences for undergraduate students.

A Collaborative Practicum Course

In 1996, the University of California plans to underwrite a cooperative venture involving researchers and undergraduates at its Irvine campus, the Boys' and Girls' Club, and Pio Pico School. Through the UCI Department of Education, undergraduate students may enroll in a practicum course to learn strategies to work with at-risk children. They will study issues of cultural diversity and literacy, engage in field research, and do volunteer community service for the students at Pio Pico. The vehicles to accomplish this collaboration are the principal, the faculty (who previously established volunteer support systems for students), and the staff of the club.

Before deciding upon teaching as a profession, university students will have an opportunity to engage in an "intergenerational" teaching strategy (Bissell, Charlton, & Mirón, 1996). The college students, pairing with Santa Ana high school students, will serve as mentors and tutors in computer activities established at the club. Thus, Pio Pico students, already socialized into the "self-discipline" goals of the club, may interact with older role models from their own neighborhoods as well as successful university students. The younger students will be able to see the cause-and-effect link between the activities at the club and the possibility of enrolling in college. Success in high school, then, potentially becomes a ticket to crossing the cultural and social border from gang member to college graduate.

The opportunity to move out of the poverty of the barrio or ghetto, leaving behind a life of gang violence, has theoretical and practical overtones very similar to the student interviews cited in Chapter 1. Whether through the legacy of the civil rights movement and its attendant demands for quality public education or, in the absence of this legacy, through new collaborative organizations, intervention strategies are essential to help multicultural students perceive that they are respected and cared for (Anfara & Mirón, 1996; Beck, 1994).

Rebuilding Community With Teamwork

Pio Pico's educational partnership (one of six) with the Boys' and Girls' Club of Santa Ana helps fulfill the vision of the school:

Education takes team work. We envision our school as the hub of our neighborhood. As such, we are constantly tapping into available resources which support our goals and objectives. At the same time, we are looking for ways in which we can assist our students in making positive contributions toward improving their immediate environment and the world at large. (Santa Ana Unified School District, 1995, p. 1)

Creating an organizational structure in which students can make positive contributions to their neighborhood sends a powerful message: Students are worthy human beings; despite their disadvantages in life, they can help persons in need. Constructive after-school programs obviously shelter children from the allure of gang life. Second, and perhaps more significant, as students mature they can become role models for younger counterparts. Not only is self-esteem fostered—in itself a powerful antidote to discrimination—but students also begin to view themselves in a wider social context. By engaging in routine activities that contribute to the quality of city life, they can broaden their academic goals, moving to the higher plateau of creating a better place to live. To paraphrase Peter McLaren (1993), students can thus create culture.

Obviously, such attitudes are not established overnight. Leadership is needed from principals to help redefine the greater purpose of schools situated in low-income minority neighborhoods. The daily routines of classroom life, what McLaren (1993) calls the "pedagogical encounter" (p. 3), also need constant nurturing from teachers. In this way, educators serve dual ends: (1) to increase self-esteem by providing students with a relevant curriculum and a voice in their own learning; and (2) through community service activities, to send symbolic messages that *students can exercise agency*—that is, they can make a positive contribution. This application of the theory of "critical pedagogy" (McLaren & Leonard, 1993) is concisely summarized in Pio Pico's motto: "A caring community of learners."

Principal Magsaysay has capitalized on the opportunity for restructuring afforded by the Santa Ana Unified School District. In Grades K through 3, her school offers a bilingual program, a rarity given the efforts of the majority Republican Congress to institute English-only policies. School leaders express the process values of communication, community, and aesthetic intelligence by being mindful to provide employment skills for a global economy, while remaining sensitive to the area's diverse, Latino-majority population. Maxcy (1995a) writes, "In stark contrast to the chaos of schools in some inner-city settings, leaders must see ways to critically appraise the diverse and discordant with an eye to the growth of conjoint and cooperative living [read: *collaboration*]" (p. 13). This sensitivity, and responsibility to act on the values of pluralistic democracy, is evident in the following passage:

> Our attendance area is made up of two streets, Highland and Brook, which contain over-crowded and rundown apartments. This is a 'port-of entry' neighborhood for many recently arrived families from all over Latin America, principally from Mexico and El Salvador. Spanish is the primary language of 98% of the students. Most of their parents have had less than four years of schooling themselves. In most households, both parents are working, usually for less than minimum wage. These are very needy families who cannot afford health or child care. Ninety-seven percent of our students participate in federally-funded breakfast and lunch programs. *Our teaching staff was selected on the basis of our commitment and willingness to work collaboratively with the community*, the district and the university to establish, develop and strive to achieve a shared vision for our school community. After much dialogue and collaboration, we have committed ourselves to this mission: to develop lifelong thinkers and learners who are eager and well-prepared to make positive contributions in a diverse global community. (Santa Ana Unified School District, 1995, p. 2, emphasis added)

The Success of Project Cleanup

The teachers and administrators at Pio Pico quickly discovered one unmet community need during the process of school restructuring—safety. The neighborhood, described above as one of the densest in the country, was not safe for children. The leadership of the school listened intently to parents who unanimously voiced concern for their children and for the neighborhood surrounding the school.

In response, Operación Liempieza (Project Cleanup) was launched. The principal forged a collaborative venture with four partners: the Santa Ana police and fire departments; Santa Ana Unified School District Building Services; and Home Base of Santa Ana, a voluntary neighborhood watch program. This sent a positive message to residents of Highland and Brook streets "that students and families on Highland and Brook Streets *do* care about improving the deplorable conditions in which they live and they want the drug and gang activity to cease" (Santa Ana Unified School District, 1995, p. 3).

Operación Liempieza has sponsored 4 neighborhood cleanup days since the school opened in 1991. A concrete outcome of this effort was the founding of the Pico Neighborhood Association out of the Parent Safety Committee. This group consists of apartment owners, managers of apartment buildings, and school family representatives from each residential building on Highland and Brook. By adhering to the process values of critical pragmatism, the school has accomplished the following results: a 48% reduction in reported crime and no school vandalism in the 1993-1995 academic years, "including no tagging or graffiti" (Santa Ana Unified School District, 1995, p. 3). Furthermore, the school district team assigned to building a new school observed that this construction project is the first one ever to report no theft or destruction of district property.

The outreach into the community to address parents' concerns has, in turn, resulted in tangible benefits for the school and staff. Participation in monthly PTA meetings stands at a remarkable 85% and there has been 100% participation in parent report card conferences. Overall, "parents report that they feel their concerns, such as safety, are being addressed and that they feel included in the processes of school and neighborhood improvement" (Santa Ana Unified School District, 1995, p. 3).

The cleanup project has had a positive effect on the instructional program at Pio Pico. Students "tackle real world problems" in an action-oriented curriculum. This program is implemented through three overlapping teams in Grades K-2, 2-4, and 4-5. Students and community members, especially parents, provide continuous feedback via weekly meetings. These teams voice a consistent question: "What is it that we want our students to Do . . . and Why?" (Santa Ana Unified School District, 1995, p. 3).

The focus on meeting the needs of the cultural-linguistic minority population is embedded in the instructional goals of the school. By simultaneously addressing the concerns of parents about safe neighborhoods and by attending to specific academic needs, the school truly has done something to boast about.

We realize the need to address the whole child. The physical, developmental, familial, cultural, socioeconomic, emotional and environmental realities of our students must impact the instructional and support programs we provide. We do not see these realities as negatives. Rather, we strive to capitalize on all that our students bring with them: a rich cultural and linguistic heritage, a strong survival instinct and a will to learn and to be active participants in the betterment of their world. An integral part of our planning and rethinking is our commitment to ourselves and our community to provide a quality bilingual education for all of our students. We strive to develop the students' home language while building a strong foundation of English language. Eighty percent of our students are in bilingual classrooms with credentialed bilingual teachers. Twenty percent of our students are in English Immersion classrooms where Sheltered English strategies are incorporated. (Santa Ana Unified School District, 1995, pp. 3-4)

In conclusion, we can review the powerful messages embedded in the stories of these two community-based partnerships—Friends of NOCCA and the Boys' and Girls' Club of Santa Ana. The most significant message is that in times of educational and social need, garnering community support is essential. The new building for the New Orleans Center for Creative Arts as well as the linguistic needs of the native Spanish-speaking children at Pio Pico School both have demanded high levels of trust and involvement from the school community and surrounding neighborhoods. The collaborative process—another process value germane to the practice of critical pragmatism—signals an emerging shift in the purpose of schools to meet local community needs. In the remaining chapters, I will spell out what this shift might entail as public schools seek to resist discrimination and institutional racism through reconstruction.

Notes

1. Throughout its 20-year history, the New Orleans Free School, a school of "choice" for at-risk students in Uptown New Orleans, has struggled to keep intact its organizational structure and independence as a magnet school. In 1990, during one of the worst school system budget crises in

recent history, the school mobilized neighborhood associations to pressure the school board to keep the school open. Principal Robert Ferris won this victory for the integrity and survival of the school by forming a powerful alliance of parents, neighborhood leaders, university faculty, and allies on the New Orleans City Council.

2. Capital outlay monies are generated by bonds authorized by state legislatures to finance highway construction, new government buildings, and, in schools, computer equipment. Rarely has the legislature in any state authorized state monies for the purpose of building new high schools. A notable exception to this informal rule is Proposition 203 (The Omnibus Education Construction Act, a $3 billion school construction bond proposal) that the California legislature placed before the voters on March 26, 1996.

3. The center's unique enrollment policies contributed to this reputation. Any qualified student in a nine-parish region—from private or public high schools—was accepted for its half-day professional arts training program. Students from parishes other than Orleans Parish were charged tuition, which kept the numbers of students from outside Orleans Parish relatively low. At the same time, school insiders complained that not enough low-income minority students were accepted.

4. Interview with the executive director of the Boys' and Girls' Club, November 1, 1995, Santa Ana, California.

5. Data provided by the U.S. Department of Education indicate that high-income neighborhoods have about four times as many after-school activities as low-income neighborhoods. See U.S. Department of Education (1994, September), *Building Community Partnerships for Learning*. Washington, DC: United States Government Printing Office, p. 28.

Making City
Government an Ally

Why are the words *government* and *government schools* so "disrespected" these days? Although President Clinton and the more moderate members of Congress still recognize that government at all levels provides a significant role in maintaining the quality of life, gone are the days when "the people" automatically looked to government for answers. Indeed, in many walks of life, this institution is seen as the *source* of, not the solution to, social woes.

In this chapter, I take a different approach. I illustrate with examples from city government the viewpoint that school leaders should form alliances with community leaders. For it was not always the case that society at large eschewed government when it came to resolving practical day-to-day problems. I demonstrate how political and policy partnerships can alleviate the pervasive ills of discrimination and institutional racism. By forging such alliances with leaders in local government, principals and teachers will find that their vision of equity and equality in public schools may more quickly become a reality.

Separation of City and Public School Government

Before laying out my rationale for this type of merger, I need to trace the history of how government came to be viewed as a menace.

In big city school districts, the private sector, and in particular elites in corporations and industry, worked hard to divorce the governance of schools from the governance of cities (Katz, 1971; Tyack, 1974). This phenomenon, over time, led to a separation of the public services of schooling from the delivery of social services for children and youth.

For our purposes, this division of power, seen as the governance of schools versus the governance of cities, is best illustrated in the office of the mayor. The main consequence of such "institutional divorce" was the removal of the mayor from the political and policy concerns of the schools. Many reformers viewed this removal as something positive. Mayors in large cities such as Chicago, for example, had acquired the reputation of overly controlling the local school board and unduly interfering with the office of the school superintendent (Peterson, 1981). In short, reformers wanted to take the politics of the mayor's political machine out of the affairs of the schools.

Of course, as reformers in the 1930s soon discovered, it is impossible to remove politics from public education. Moreover, the naive alienation of the governance of schools from that of the city meant the capacity of the mayor's office to bring needed financial, organizational and, yes, even political, resources to school districts was virtually wasted. The governance of education remained political—that is, "endemic to the profession itself" (Garvin & Young, 1994, p. 94). Mayors Daly and Walmsley, in the cities of Chicago and New Orleans, respectively, turned their attention—and considerable resources—toward matters they could directly influence.[1] Garvin and Young (1994) expand on this change:

> In a move seen as progressive at the turn of the century, education was turned over to professional educators and removed from the influence of the world of city politics. Not only was this the de-coupling of schools from city government, it was also the harbinger of schools being de-coupled from the rest of the community. This de-coupling led to a restructuring of the concept of the neighborhood school. Such schools had often served as the hub of activities that were characteristic of particular communities and particular groups of people. [Within this model] schools became residential anchor points, *serving not only as places of learning for children, but as focal points where community health care*

could be given, political meetings could be held, and information deemed essential to the body politic dispersed. (p. 94, emphasis added)

Quality neighborhood schools historically have played a strong role in reducing discrimination in society. Researchers have noted an overriding factor present where there is an inequality in school outcomes, along with a diminishing of life chances based on race, ethnicity, gender, and social class (in other words, discrimination)—there is a greater degree of social isolation in proportion to the degree of residential segregation (Garvin, 1994; Haymes, 1995; Wilson, 1987). Put simply, the more racially isolated, and thus segregated, students' residences become in the community, the greater the discrimination and racism. Targeting discrimination in schools, then, is inseparable from the process of alleviating discrimination in housing policies.

In the next section, I show how the Chicago School Reform Act (1988) caused many positive changes in school governance. However, the focus of this major policy change was still too narrowly defined in terms of improved student outcomes, to the potential detriment of the quality of life in neighborhoods, especially distressed ones. Only by reconstructing the vision and mission of public schooling to address the dual problem of school and residential discrimination can these problems be effectively addressed.

Redefining School Reform

Mayor Richard Daly, Jr., has worked with the Chicago School Board and local school communities to provide transitional steps to redefine the intention of school reform in Chicago. I want to take his approach a step further and illustrate how teachers, principals, and now parents can coalesce with city government to eliminate discrimination in neighborhood schools. By working together, we can move toward reducing discrimination in all of society. First, I need to review how public schools have suffered because of the structural, political, and, for lack of a better term, "identity" problems associated with school reform in Chicago.

The original Chicago School Reform Act of 1988 (the Act) did not authorize the mayor to reorganize the central office administrative bureaucracy. Rather, the Act allowed for the election of local school councils (LSC) in order to have day-to-day authority over school-level policy. The LSCs are composed of eleven members: six parents, two teachers, two community residents, and the school principal. In concept, the LSC may hire and fire the principal, set school budgets, and approve the curriculum. Structurally, this means that parents have the greatest voice in school policy. This practice is brand new; prior to 1995, parents did not have this much authority and visibility.

In a focused empirical study of the implementation of the Act, Lewis and Nakagawa (1995) examined closely the inner workings of the LSCs. In particular, they sought to understand the role of public school parents in the policy deliberations of the LSCs. The authors conceptualized these roles as either "enabling" or "empowering." Their research documents the outworn pattern of parents as enablers of professionally driven school policy.

Parents as Enablers

Parents of school children traditionally have assumed what Kathryn Nakagawa (1995) has called an enabling role. This role is structured through a host of parental involvement policies and op-portunities designed to support the school and assist professionals such as the principal and classroom teachers. The enablement model has its roots in the professionalization of education:

> Although nineteenth-century American public schools were subject to community desires and constraints, schools required more formal organization as the demographics of cities changed, and professionals came to dominate the direction of education. (Tyack, 1974; cited in Nakagawa, 1995, p. 5)

Nakagawa notes that the enabling model of parental involve-ment was embedded in the ideology and discourse of the "Progres-sive Education Movement" in the 1920s and 1930s. The author quotes from a pamphlet published by the Association for the Ad-vancement of Progressive Education to make this linkage clear:

> It is the duty of the parents to know what the school is doing and why; and to find out the most effective way to co-operate. It is the duty of the school to help the parents to make available all

the resources of the school that can give information or help to the home. (Cremin, 1962, p. 245, cited in Nakagawa, 1995, p. 5)

Unfortunately, the original Chicago School Reform Act of 1988 outlined opportunities for participation that had the unintended consequence of providing parents with poor information and little training. Parents, too, often manifested a self-image that limited their involvement to one of enablement. One mother from the northwest side of Chicago put forth this issue squarely: the principal should establish the budget.

[The Principal] did most of the work because *he really is the one who knows the most.* And then we'd discuss it and improve, or give ideas or whatever. But he did most of it. Which is really what—how I think it should be anyway. I mean, I'm not about to start fooling with the budget. He would always ask us, but we would pretty much stick to what he had. [S]ometimes people on the board felt they had to put their two cents in about something. . . . when maybe the best person to handle a certain thing would have been just the principal. (Lewis & Nakagawa, 1995, p. 136, emphasis added)

Clearly, some parents strongly prefer to let school professionals control matters of policy. Others, as we shall see below, prefer to act on their own, a form of legally sanctioned empowerment. In any case, the nature of the *technical* information about school policy—the budget, curriculum, school improvement—appears to be an overriding factor in determining which of the two models of involvement parents ultimately will assume.

Self-Empowered Parents

It seems that not all parents are fully able to empower themselves, even when such measures as the Act are in place. But a growing number of parents exploit the structural opportunities at hand to decide school policy. Somehow, their life histories provide them with the historical experience of making the system work. They do not see themselves as "victims." For example, the mother of one of the students we interviewed from Neighborhood High was ready to take the issue of her daughter's grades to the local school board if it meant that her daughter's diploma was in jeopardy (Mirón & Lauria, 1995). She partly learned this tactic during the civil rights movement in the Deep South. Nakagawa writes:

> Current school decentralization movements and school-based management reforms have included this type of parent involvement—usually some governing board on which parents will serve. . . . Parent involvement on local school councils is often a requirement attached to federal moneys, such as Chapter 1. . . . However, Chicago marks the most drastic test of empowerment as parents are given majority policy-making responsibility at the school site. (1995, p. 7)

Although some parents may lack the formal training and informational resources to take substantive roles in school policy, these constraints do not foil them. Yet conflict between school professionals and parents may be exacerbated when the issue of expertise arises. The following excerpt from an interview with a parent in the LSC in Chicago is illustrative:

> [T]he teachers felt, "We are the professionals, we can do this, we know about the character of this school." But then there was a real big group of the LSC that felt, "This is why we're here in the first place, we're not going to rubber stamp anything." (Nakagawa, 1995, p. 19)

These self-empowered parents were able to use the structure of the LSC mandated by state law (a majority vote on the Council) to influence school-level policy. Disagreement apparently arose from the question of "who knows best," based on the perceived dichotomy between parent and teacher knowledge of school improvement. A critical-pragmatic model, based on communication and collaboration, would instead focus policy on making a concrete difference in the everyday lives of students and teachers. Working in concert to erase discrimination in schools by alleviating the pernicious effects of discrimination in housing and other services is one such way to concretely redefine the goal of collaboration.

Reconciling Conflict

How can we reconcile these two apparently opposing models of parental involvement? Nakagawa (1995) summarizes Epstein's (1993) concerns.

> The shift from enablement to empowerment creates a conflict in terms of the parent-school relationship. . . . On one level, when it is assumed that parents and community members are as capable as teachers and the principal to make decisions about schooling, professional expertise diminishes in importance. Empowerment models that are mandated by policy thus often result in a natural opposition in the school rather than a partnership. (Nakagawa, 1995, p. 26)
>
> On another level, parents must reconcile their traditional ennoblement roles with the new empowerment roles. A tension may be created for the individual parent between conforming with already accepted school roles and learning to confront and challenge the school through the new parent status. (Nakagawa, 1995, p. 7)

I have already alluded to the divisive political struggle over the power to define knowledge about schooling. Teachers and principals understandably feel that their professional training has equipped them with the expertise to guide the schooling process—what works best for teaching and learning. Habermas (1970) says that such decisions by professionals may satisfy technical interests, but in the process, the concept of human needs of students within a caring school is often forgotten. Moreover, students who have been discriminated against at school typically live in neighborhoods characterized by social and racial isolation. Again, we come full circle to the importance of a shared vision of the role of the school in improving the overall quality of life for students.

When parents and teachers become partners in matters of daily living, improvements in the behavior of students and in the quality of life in the neighborhoods where they live will result. The leadership process in schools is the way to reconcile the conflicts between the enabling and empowering models of parental involvement.

In the next section, I will illustrate the strategies by which local government can be brought in as an ally of parents, teachers, and principals to refocus the dialogue on the concrete problems of discrimination and institutional racism. I first return to the Chicago School Reform Act and then draw upon recent changes in the city charter in New Orleans.

Transitional Change—Reinventing Central Office

The original Chicago School Reform Act of 1988 became the Amendatory Reform Act on July 1, 1995. Chicago Mayor Daly was given a mandate to appoint a new, smaller school board and revamp the central administration. The greatly reduced school board—a five-member board of trustees—began to "set the financial house in order and direct resources to classrooms . . ." (Cowlishaw, 1995). Perhaps even more significant, the mayor was asked to revamp the management team in the central office. The concrete result has been that rather than functioning as a "professional enclave," the district is becoming a "unit of local government" (Hess, 1995, p. 28).

The Illinois state legislature, working in coalition with the mayor, the Chicago Board of Education, citizen groups, the governor, the University of Illinois at Chicago, and the Illinois Business Education Coalition, has effectively restored mayoral politics at the level of district management. Hess (1995) writes:

> [T]he team appointed by Mayor Richard M. Daly has brought a very different notion of school district management with it. Not only were the top management positions exempted from educational certification requirements, the criteria for the positions virtually eliminated those "ed admin" types. In addition, because both the managers and the smaller, five-member board were both directly appointed by the mayor, neither group was protected from direct partisan, political influence. *The whole intent of the Amendatory Act was to restore political responsibility for, and control over, the school system's management.* (p. 28, emphasis added)

Scandalous! Critics argue that political machines, such as those within the mayor's office, should keep out of the "business of education." What these "good government" critics often forget, however, is that career education professionals (superintendents) are politicians as well. The political orientation of top managers in the central office, as Hess (1995) reminds us, is toward the maintenance of professional enclaves that "became unresponsive, not only to parents and citizens, but to professionals at the school level as well" (p. 28). My own research confirms this criticism, as principals I interviewed complained repeatedly that the central office doesn't care about the schools or the students in them (Murry, Bogotch, & Mirón, 1995).

From my cursory review of the literature on the politics of education, it is clear that an unintended political consequence of the progressive movement in education was the institutionalization of unresponsive professional enclaves. Indeed, as Peterson (1981) has theorized, professional norms in the central office have worked merely to perpetuate the organizational culture and upward mobility of the people who work there. These professionals have no political constituents per se—they tend mostly to help each other.

The Best of City Hall Culture

How has Mayor Daly reinvented the culture of the schools' central office? In short, he has transformed it into the culture of city hall. As Hess (1995) writes,

[T]he fact that this culture is the culture of "city halls" is what is important. What distinguishes this team is the conception it holds that the district is a unit of local government, not a professional enclave. Under this concept, decisions must reflect what is politically required and what is politically possible, rather than what is professionally judged to be correct. (p. 22)

Based on a political model partially dependent upon, and supported by, the mayor, educational policy making in Chicago has radically changed. Central office managers, as well as the board of trustees, must be responsive to constituents and consult with leaders in the local communities. They find it important to maintain ongoing open relations with the news media to gain support for public policy, and even work with state legislators from the opposing political party. Compromise and consensus building have become operative terms, leaving no room for inflexible, even if expert, judgment.

For example, the new administration early on tackled the problem of overcrowded schools in one of the city's predominantly Hispanic communities. The new model of governance refocused attention on solving political problems—and on how to respond to Hispanic students' needs and those of their families. The mayor was represented on the board of trustees by his former chief of staff and in the central office by his former budget manager, who now serves as chief executive officer of the school district. Together, they worked with the Hispanic community on the northwest side of Chicago to reopen a high school and thus relieve overcrowding in classrooms.

The plan for the neighborhood, however, had the unanticipated negative result of reducing Hispanic enrollment in the predominantly African American schools on the west side.[2] Hispanic and African American residents proposed an alternative to the plan put forward by the central office. The west-side school, Creiger, became a multisite facility housing several new smaller schools, a policy sought by the administration. Hess (1995) concluded that "recognizing failure and walking away from it so quickly is an approach that would have been impossible for professionalized bureaucrats, with their self important 'expert judgment,' bolstering, and blockading every decision" (p. 22).

Potential Problems to Consider

Of course, the transformation of school governance to "city hall culture" has its problems. The most immediate is embedded in Hess's (1995, p. 22) description of the culture of "self-importance" in professional enclaves at central office. This behavior violates the tenets of critical pragmatism, with its emphasis on the process values of communication, community, and aesthetic intelligence. Moreover, remember that effective community-based partnerships (see Chapter 6) also include yet another major process value, collaboration. It appears from early accounts in Chicago that *political collaboration* is indeed present, but at the expense of the input and involvement of professionals at individual schools. At best, the process seems quite limited, if only for the simple reason that without significant attention to the needs of principals and teachers, disharmony will result. If left unchecked, this could bring negative public relations, a most unwelcome possibility for the mayor's team.[3]

The problem is that the pendulum may have swung too far in the other direction. I want to be especially clear here. I firmly believe in the potential of pluralistic democracies such as ours to responsively meet the needs of their citizenry. Public schools should work no differently. A political climate that might pit classroom teachers (and perhaps school administrators) against the board of trustees and the mayor's administrative team may produce, at best, short-term solutions. Even if minority student needs are met, without support from professionals in all sectors of the education community students might experience a subsequent backlash in the classroom. In other words, political victories would become a zero-sum game. Together we must rectify every situation that potentially pits teachers against central office managers. I present an alternative scenario based upon case study data from New Orleans to underscore the value of collaboration.

A Win-Win Alternative?

During his campaign for mayor of New Orleans, Marc Morial spoke about becoming the first "education mayor." Like most politicians, Morial realized the depth of public concern about improving public schools. Indeed, his father, considered one of the great mayors in the history of the city, had fought a hard battle to gain mayoral appointments to the Orleans Parish School Board.[4] Ernest "Dutch" Morial lost this fight.

When Marc Morial took office in April, 1994, he proposed an education liaison with the office of the mayor. He organized a broad-based 50-member task force whose major policy recommendation was to endorse the call for this collaboration.[5] A conference cosponsored by the Metropolitan Area Committee (a nonprofit civic leadership group) and the University of New Orleans closely examined the historical relationships between the mayor and the Orleans Parish School Board. It was discovered that the school district prospered when the mayor was substantially involved in the politics and financing of public education in the city. Conversely, in the absence of this involvement, the school district declined (Devore & Logsdon, 1991).

In early May, less than a month after taking office, Morial addressed a meeting of the Orleans Parish School Board. This was the first appearance ever by a mayor before the school board. Morial pledged cooperation between his office and the new superintendent of schools, Dr. Morris Holmes. Moreover, Morial praised the then-president of the board, Cheryl Cramer, who, along with the president of the United Teachers of New Orleans, cochaired the task force.[6] The mayor wanted to convey publicly a message of cooperation, especially in light of the mutual capital needs (streets, school buildings) of the city and the school system.

Case study data summarizing the new political relationships between the mayor and the school board in New Orleans reveal the spirit of collaboration—not confrontation. The mayor did not attempt to "take over" the school board, although that was certainly a concern of professionals in the central office enclave. Rather, he pledged a climate of teamwork to address the problems of chronic underfunding.

Two examples of collaboration and professional teamwork illustrate the concrete steps that school principals can take. Working in conjunction with their teaching staff, administrators can secure government help to reduce the pernicious effects of discrimination. Below I describe the details surrounding a federal grant application submitted by the city of New Orleans for status as an "Empowerment Zone" and the amendment to the city charter to establish "cooperative ventures."

Seeking Federal Recognition

The city Department of Policy and Planning organized an impressive group of civic leaders who volunteered to assemble an Empowerment Zone grant application for $10 million.[7] Unfortunately, New Orleans was not one of the six cities nationwide to be awarded a grant. However, the approach taken by the city in producing its proposal to provide a comprehensive array of social services in education, health care, police protection, and medical assistance (Warner, 1994) is worth reviewing.

The federal grant application was coordinated with the development of a comprehensive strategic plan for the city. The broad philosophical vision of this plan directly links the future health and growth of the city to the quality of public schools.

Basic education lies at the heart of individual and community capacity building and empowerment. Hence it lies at the heart of this plan. It is no secret that the public school system in New Orleans is one of the weakest in the country, largely due to the State's regressive tax structure and resulting chronic under-funding. Yet without a well-educated work force, the [Empowerment] Zone will lack the ability to create and take advantage of economic opportunities; and without economic opportunities, the initiatives designed to improve housing and reduce crime will come to naught. *The future of the Orleans Parish School District is, in many ways, the future of all New Orleans.* (City of New Orleans, 1994, p. vi, emphasis added)

Good public schools help build strong communities. Healthy communities value good public schools. The possibilities to realize these reciprocal connections make up the strategic plan. In addition, "The proper focus of the plan is the embodiment of the City's future, its youth" (City of New Orleans, 1994, pp. i-1).

The long-term goal of the plan, as articulated in the Empowerment Zone application, was designed to reestablish the linkages among neighborhood schools, youth and family services, and the quality of life in distressed neighborhoods. If the grant was funded, revenues would be available to extend the hours of neighborhood schools so they could be used as centers for community services.[8] The city also intended to establish neighborhood youth councils to implement after-school and summer peer-tutoring programs. Moreover, training and education funds would assist young people in finding summer jobs and year-round employment. Finally, $7.3 million in federal funds was to be earmarked for student health services. The authors of the Empowerment Zone application articulated this comprehensive, community-based approach:

Educational initiatives and linkages between education and such topics as entrepreneurship, job preparedness, health care, early childhood development, family support and the arts permeate the plan. . . . Successful schools are those in which the surrounding neighborhood takes an active interest. Within the Zone, increasing this level of interest and the involvement of residents will be essential to not only improving the quality and responsiveness of the schools but also to better integrating education delivery with other aspects of community life. (City of New Orleans, 1994, pp. vi-vii)

The city of New Orleans ultimately lost out to politically stronger cities such as Los Angeles and New York, but due to this experience, many students—especially those who have felt victimized by discrimination—have been assisted. Through federally funded community service (see below), individuals have found a way to feel more self-empowered and see their plight as inseparable from the plight of their neighbors. I will next show how, by acting in concert, voters are improving the quality of neighborhoods and reducing discrimination, both inside and outside of their schools.

The Appeal of Cooperative Ventures

Although the city of New Orleans did not receive federal Empowerment Zone status, it did attain a less prestigious, and less financially palatable, category of urban poverty classification. The new collaborative relationships the mayor had forged with the Orleans Parish School Board and the superintendent of schools also helped secure a combined windfall of half a billion dollars to pay for local infrastructure improvements (street repairs, etc.) and school renovations. The new partnership between city government and the school district is best illustrated in the city charter with an amendment known as the "cooperative ventures" measure.

Embracing conflict. As a participant-observer (see Anderson, Herr, & Nihlen, 1994, pp. 130-138), I chaired a subcommittee on intergovernmental relations. One of the key tasks under my purview was to analyze ways that city government and the public school system, and in particular the local school board, could work more closely together. My cochair had been active in the Metropolitan Area Committee's education task force and regularly met with the superintendent and members of the school board. She was not keen on the issue of city-school cooperation when she learned that we were to investigate the area of "capital needs."

Within the school district, the word *capital* has one specific meaning—the financing of computer equipment. At city hall, however, the word has signified either street repair and improvements or facilities for community development, namely libraries and police substations. The chair of the mayor's charter revision task force had a vision that the school district and city government could plan together that would suit them both. One example he cited repeatedly had to do with the location of libraries. The city and the school district could cooperatively plan—and finance—public libraries that would be adjacent to schools in distressed residential neighborhoods. These schools could then gain new libraries they would not otherwise be able to finance, and the city could open facilities that would be equally attractive to neighborhood residents.[9]

But there was still a conflict to be dealt with. My cochair had recently negotiated a proposal with central office administrators to let school-site councils allocate funds for the purchase of computers (part of a school-based budgeting experiment). Previously, parents and business partners affiliated with the Metropolitan Area Committee school partnership program had been hampered by centralized purchasing procedures in the district office. For example, if a business or the PTA wanted to donate computers, it might be months before district administrators approved the gift.

Thus the specter of mayoral control haunted community leaders. They did not want to see their hard work to gain school-site budgeting autonomy possibly give way to a new form of bureaucracy. What steps led to a change in attitude? The solution lay in a change in language. The meaning of the word *capital* needed redefinition. This redefinition would be accomplished by exact (legal) language in the charter amendment specifying in great detail what the cooperative endeavor would and would not facilitate in the way of capital planning.

The power of language. The school district constituency of the charter advisory committee supported changing the language of the amendment from "capital improvements" (read: computers) to "public works" (read: school buildings, libraries, police stations). I vividly recall that as the amendment came up for a final vote before the committee, my cochair was jubilant to hear the news that the wording would be changed. The final amendment reads:

> The City of New Orleans may enter into cooperative endeavors with the state or its political subdivisions or political corporations, with the United States or its agencies, or with any public or private association, corporation or individual with regard to the procurement and development of immovable property, joint planning and implementation activities, joint funding initiatives, and other similar activities in support of public education,

community development, housing rehabilitation, economic growth, and other public purposes. (City of New Orleans, 1995, p. 158)

Although the charter amendment does not name the Orleans Parish School Board explicitly, this body is one of the intended "political corporations." I had long conversations with the chair of the advisory committee, David Marcello, who expressed strong interest in having city government and the school district conduct the joint planning, siting of schools and libraries, and even the location of new police substations adjacent to schools with dangerously high crime rates. In fact, Marcello, a former city attorney and director of the Public Law Center, a joint training and legal research project of Tulane and Loyola Universities, took pains to craft explicit legalese detailing how these cooperative endeavors would work. Part 2 of Section 9-314 of the amendment, approved by the New Orleans City Council and ratified by the voters, reads as follows:

> In order to further these objectives, each department and board of City government shall prepare within sixty days following the first day of each calendar year a report to the Mayor regarding opportunities for coordination between the department or board and other entities as previously enumerated in this section. Within thirty days following receipt of such reports, the Mayor shall direct such departments or boards as the Mayor deems appropriate to initiate discussions with certain specified entities relative to cooperative endeavor agreements. Each department or board so directed shall within sixty days thereafter report to the Mayor on the status of discussions regarding cooperative agreements. (City of New Orleans, 1995, p. 158)

Concrete results. What are the concrete results to date for the school district? In November, 1995, New Orleans voters joined forces and overwhelmingly passed the new city charter. More significantly, 66% of the voters were in favor of budgeting $330 million in bonds to repair school buildings. This amount falls short of the half billion dollars the school district estimated that it would need. However, the approval of the bond issue is a creditable beginning toward accomplishing the mutual goals of the city and the public schools.

How will the enactment of cooperative endeavors reduce discrimination in public schools and in segregated neighborhoods? Recent scholarship (Bondi, 1993) has suggested that cities, and central-city neighborhoods in particular, contribute to students' sense of identity and efficacy. Poor, racially segregated neighborhoods contribute greatly to students' social isolation from mainstream society (Garvin, 1994). At the same time, African American and other ethnic minority cultures that are embedded in neighborhoods such as Atlanta, Detroit, Los Angeles, New Orleans, and New York City have been highly involved in the civil rights movement. We know that minorities who overcome discrimination by members of the dominant society in turn gain a legacy of person rights (Apple, 1988) such as access to quality public schools and decent, affordable housing.

Low-income minority students in New Orleans, as a result of the bond issue jointly won by the city and the school district, will learn in better facilities. They finally will be able to change classes on rainy days without getting soaked and attend school without fear of buildings collapsing or of lead poisoning from old paint. These gains may sound like trifles to students in affluent suburban public schools or those in wealthy private schools. But to inner-city students, such accommodations are privileges that may feel special.

By reducing and eventually eliminating the *consequences of discrimination and institutional racism*, students may be in a stronger position to empower themselves. We may not be able to eliminate racist behavior entirely in the long run. However, by altering the social structures of inequality that engender the reproduction of discrimination and institutional racism—for example, by improving school facilities in segregated neighborhoods—we can attempt to level the playing field. It is important, therefore, for school administrators, principals, assistant principals, and curriculum supervisors to meet together with city hall staff and devise strategies to refurbish their schools.

Race *Does* Matter

In Chapter 6, I suggested that reactions to a person's *race* form a symbolic code of largely unspoken messages. Such messages greatly influenced the board of directors of the Friends of the New Orleans Center for Creative Arts in the successful relocation of the new arts high school. In particular, the ability of the FON leaders to collaborate with African American school board members, principals from "feeder schools," and the superintendent of schools helped dispel the reputation that the school served mostly affluent white students from Uptown New Orleans. By publicly recommitting to outreach in low-income minority neighborhoods in the city, FON was able to gain the requisite political support of the local school board. With money in hand from the State of Louisiana's capital outlay program, the leadership of FON was able to take concrete steps to relocate the school.

In the same fashion, we saw the spirit of cooperation among the New Orleans African American governmental elites who joined forces to pass a bond issue for street repairs and the renovation of public schools. Moreover, the chairman of the mayoral-appointed charter advisory committee was a white attorney, previously an executive in the administration of "Dutch" Morial, and a faculty member in elite private universities in the city. Another example of racial alliance was the development of the strategy for forging "cooperative ventures," a tack that is leading to better school facilities for the youth of New Orleans.

Apparently, the spirit of racial coalition building was lacking in the case of the Amendatory Chicago School Reform Act. Here, white politicians in the Daly administration actively chased out the previous ethnic minority school board and the mostly African American central office administrators. Upon naming the new "super board" and central office managers, Mayor Daly commented, "Business as usual is over. The special interests will have to move to the back of the line. The bureaucrats who stand in the way of change will be removed and their powers dissolved" (quoted in Bradley, 1995a, p. 3).

Already we see evidence of disgruntlement from the teachers' unions and perhaps resistance from school-level administrators. In any case, we find in Chicago much less of a "win-win" political environment. We will await further results to see if what appears to be a less racially inclusive strategy in Chicago will mean less discrimination for the thousands of African American students there.

We learn two powerful lessons from the examples in this chapter. First, as educators we must create new organizational and political structures to provide greater opportunities for students who have been oppressed by the structures that facilitate the reproduction of unequal power relations. In short, students who have grown up as victims—that is, without a sense of personal and political power—must be provided with structural opportunities to *act empowered*. This could be as simple as the opportunity to attend schools that are in the same physical condition as those of students in affluent suburbs, or in areas within the same school district where middle-class parents are able to raise money for their schools, such as in Uptown New Orleans or south Orange County, California. As a result of these good actions on their behalf, it is more likely these students will gain self-esteem and the ability to empower themselves against discrimination and institutional racism in the wider society.

Second, if we hope ever to resolve the issue of racism in schools and local communities, we must form biracial coalitions to actively work on reaching this goal. Confronting minority politicians on educational issues with threats of takeover is likely only to exacerbate racism toward individuals and increase the likelihood that more subtle forms of institutional racism will linger longer. On the other hand, if structured collaboratively, city government can become a welcome partner in working toward the ideal of resisting discrimination and racism, both in terms of neutralizing negative attitudes and in advocating for social justice.

Notes

1. The city charter of New Orleans, as in many cities, prohibits any formal relationship between city government (the mayor and council members) and the public schools. The important exceptions are the state legislatures in Chicago and Boston (discussed in this chapter).

2. According to Hess, the plan attracted fewer than eight Latino students. See G. Alfred Hess, Jr. (1995), "Chicago's New Perspective on District Management." *Education Week*, p. 22.

3. A survey of teacher attitudes in Chicago since passage of the Amendatory Act revealed that high school teachers appeared removed from the work of school reform. On the other hand, elementary teachers appeared positive about the impact of school reform. See Ann Bradley (1995b), "Survey of Chicago Teachers Paints Uneven Portrait of Reform." *Education Week*, p. 10.

4. Since the 1920s, as part of the legacy of the Progressive Movement, the Louisiana state constitution prohibited the mayor from any formal relationship with the school board.

5. I was a member of this task force and chaired the subcommittee that made the recommendation and spelled out the functions of the new education liaison.

6. Morial later tapped Cramer to head up the reorganized Private Industry Council, which funneled federal dollars to education and training programs for youth in the inner city.

7. For a detailed description of the consensus-building process, see Louis F. Mirón (1995), "Pushing the Boundaries of Urban School Reform: Linking Student Outcomes to Community Development." *Journal for a Just and Caring Education,* 1(1), pp. 80-98.

8. This extension was included in the plan to relocate the New Orleans Center for Creative Arts (see Chapter 6). FON would keep its doors open in the evening to provide local musicians and artists with space to practice and give public performances.

9. I witnessed this phenomenon in my neighborhood in New Orleans. The city opened a new library in the Broadmoor area, a racially mixed, mostly middle-class area. The library was an attractive facility and was located only a couple of blocks from a neighborhood elementary school. When it opened, the community immediately noticed an improvement. An attractive, refurbished building, well lighted and available for neighborhood meetings, had brightened the area!

Cultivating an Ethics of the Heart

Two articles printed in the *Los Angeles Times* in March, 1996, dramatically reveal the paradoxes within the legal system.[1] Both articles deal with the issues surrounding illegal immigration and point to U. S. constitutional law and congressional legislation as dominating factors that have determined the parameters of discrimination in the public schools. They also uncover a disturbing societal trend: Ethical practices are increasingly being shaped legally, rather than with the sense of compassion, care, and forgiveness[2] that scholars argue schools must develop (Beck, 1994; Noddings, 1992, 1994; Sergiovanni, 1996; Starratt, 1994). As I shall show in this chapter, such discursive practice (Cherryholmes, 1988) has contributed to a paucity of moral leadership in public schools.

Punishing the Children

Prohibiting Government Grants

In Garden Grove, California, Principal Carolyn Reichert and teachers at Lampson Elementary School, where 75% of the children live in poverty and more than 50% speak only limited English, have obtained funding to provide for needed social services such as medical assistance and parenting classes. This funding derives in large part from a $50,000 "Heart to Heart" grant from the state and $25,000 in private funds from the Weingart Foundation. The program, admin-istered by the school, serves more than 30 community groups, assists about 300 students per year (or one third of the total enrollment), and provides free counseling, medical and dental care, plus many other services for students (Seo, 1996, p. A17). This exemplifies what can result from using the kinds of collaborative strategies and adminis-trative leadership practices detailed and advocated in this book.

The school, however, seems to be a victim of its own success. Many other schools in the district are now seeking grants to provide for similar social and health services. The Orange School District Board of Trustees' president, Martin Jacobson, sees this trend as problematic:

> If a school wants to be aggressive about referring families to community clinics, I'm all for that. . . . The big issue for me is setting up a facility on campus. I believe it takes away campus space and takes the focus away from education. (quoted in Seo, 1996, p. A17)

The board of trustees wants to prohibit schools from applying for grants to pay for such services. I will return to an analysis of the Orange County situation, but first, a parallel story follows concern-ing the vote in the U. S. House of Representatives to deny free public education to children of illegal immigrants.

Identifying Illegal Students

On March 21, 1996, the House approved legislation (on a 333-87 vote) permitting states to deny public education to students who are in the country illegally. The bill, if passed by the Senate, also would reduce public benefits for legal immigrants. In this compromise ac-tion, seen by opponents as partial to business, the House has pro-posed two types of immigrants—*legal* and *illegal*. The former cate-gory acknowledges that "those who come into the country legally help the nation's economy" (Lacey, 1996, p. A16). If the bill passes, classroom teachers will be largely responsible for executing the "sur-veillance" required to identify illegal students and for notifying the Immigration and Naturalization Service to deport them.[3]

In some respects, this legislation parallels Proposition 187, the initiative California voters approved in 1995 that bans free public schooling to students who are in the country illegally and in the process has become a political rallying cry. For example, during his brief stint at running for the presidency, California Governor Pete Wilson employed illegal-immigrant bashing so frequently that it became the rhetorical centerpiece of his campaign. And because presidential candidate Bob Dole has made clear his own endorsement of the national legislation, Proposition 187—and its potentially harsh treatment of the children of illegal immigrants—has moved to center stage in the national political arena.

Liberal activists and constitutional scholars decry the possibility that there might be an amendment allowing states the legal discretion to deny free public schooling to illegal immigrants. One activist says, "This raises the level of acceptability of all kinds of overt and virulent immigrant-bashing. . . . It is the worst kind of bullying because it goes after the most innocent and vulnerable population among us."[4] If successful, the House amendment could nullify the legal precedent established when the U. S. Supreme Court ruled in 1982 in *Plyer v. Doe* that the state of Texas must provide free public schooling to children of illegal immigrants.

A bitter irony is operative here. On the one hand, proponents of Proposition 187, and its companion legislation passed by the House, are asserting staunchly conservative values that vehemently resist the intrusion of government into private life. However, these same ideologues apparently see nothing wrong when they turn to the federal government, and potentially the U.S. Constitution, for help in denying public education and other social services to children of immigrants, both legal and illegal. As constitutional scholar Kenneth L. Karst argues, "the [Supreme Court] has been very deferential to Congress in Congress's regulation of aliens" (quoted in Pyle & McDonnell, 1996; see Note 4).

Legalizing Discrimination?

The two stories above impel me to ask a disturbing question: Are conservative forces[5] manipulating the legal system to rid "undesirable" groups (illegal immigrants) from their communities? I believe that the anecdotal, if not legal, evidence is that they are. The question is why. Let me return to the example of Lampson Elementary.

Demographic data collected by the *Los Angeles Times* (Lacey, 1996; Seo, 1996) reveal that during the past decade, the school's enrollment underwent a transformation. It changed from a majority white middle-class population to an enrollment that is mostly Latino, Asian, and black. Most of these families have such low incomes that their children are eligible for federally funded lunches. We can infer from the anecdotal data and demographic evidence that the racial-ethnic identity, as well as social class, of most of the children has contributed to the concerns of the local board of trustees. Put simply, had the school demographic profile remained consistent—that is, consisting of white middle-class families—the principal and teachers would have had a much reduced need to provide substantially more social services.

Orange County, California, is similar in culture to many other affluent suburban communities throughout the southwestern United States. It has a conservative political culture that is skeptical about big government and large institutions in general. Its well-to-do residents, therefore, disdain paying taxes that they perceive benefit people living on public assistance such as "welfare" (e.g., Aid to Families with Dependent Children [AFDC], etc.). They largely believe that a family's plight in society is a result of its own making. Citizens in Orange County generally espouse the idea of the personal responsibility and liberty of the individual.

Michael Apple (1993) argues that the phenomenon of the "New Right" has turned the principles of democracy upside down. Conservative politicians have gained control of Congress and many state legislatures throughout the country. Moreover, neopopulist movements, such as the Republican Party elites' *Contract With America*, have sought to turn over fiscal responsibility for social programs to state government and the private sector. These elites apparently have focused upon the anger and financial insecurity of working-class white Americans and have begun to enact public policies that protect individual freedom, thus undermining the civil rights of historically underrepresented minorities.[6]

My purpose here is not to examine the relative merits of political ideologies of "conservative" and "liberal" groups. Instead, I want to illustrate my theory that legal discourse is increasingly becoming a means to engender discriminatory practices in public schools. At the very least, it appears that recent educational policies and legal

decisions have had the unintended consequence of fueling immigrant bashing and of potentially harming ethnic minorities in general, many of whom are legal immigrants and native-born citizens.
Ironically, the move in Orange County, California, to prohibit schools
from applying for certain funding derives from the policies of government itself. "Government" here is the board of trustees.

In the name of individual liberty, a stance that is purportedly
against government intrusion of any kind, conservative politicians
such as those members of the Garden Grove Board of Trustees may
simultaneously invoke their authority, granted by the state constitution, to interpose into the daily practices of schools and school districts. How ironic that the principal and teacher-leaders in Lampson
Elementary did not need to draw upon state or local *education* funds
to provide these resources! Furthermore, by invoking the collaborative support of the local community and nonprofit organizations,
these leaders have vividly exhibited the "personal responsibility"
that the national electorate seems to universally support.

The move to use the law, broadly defined, to reverse strategies
such as affirmative action will likely lead to increased discriminatory
practices in public schools. For example, the reporting of suspected
illegal immigrants as set forth in Proposition 187, if upheld, will set
in motion decision making that ignores a higher moral standard of
what benefits children and families. Rather, classroom teachers may
have no realistic alternative *except* to "follow the law." We will then
be practicing an ethics dominated by legal discourse.

Are there any serious alternatives to this pessimistic realization?
I think there are. In the sections that follow, I will sketch out an ethical standard based on compassion and kindness. For I believe that
school leaders like those at Lampson Elementary are plentiful, and
we as educators will see countless more examples of affirmative
strategies to rid our schools and classrooms of discrimination for-
ever. The sobering caution is that political elites not use dominance
through legal discourse to resist making this happen.

Ultimately, legal discourse of the type cited in this chapter "re-
constructs" students' identities (Mirón, 1996). That is, racial-ethnic
minority students such as African Americans who have learned to
assert their right to quality public schooling through the legacy of
civil rights (Mirón & Lauria, 1995) may now come to feel that the law
no longer protects them. They may have no recourse against unintentional discrimination in their classroom. Worse, rather than stra-

tegically choosing to do "what they have to do" to succeed and to graduate, they may engage in self-destructive forms of resistance (McLaren, 1993; Willis, 1977). If this were to happen, these racial-ethnic minority students could lose the battle for self-empowerment.

Finally, classroom teachers may be expected to assume new professional identities, shaped in large part by legal pressures to police children and older students from families of illegal immigrants. Potentially forced to teach in the context of legal structures that deny public education, teachers may succumb to behaving at the level of "street bureaucrats" of the Immigration and Naturalization Service. Fortunately, there are more positive ways to act based on moral-ethical values that show care, respect, and compassion for students and families.

A Call for Ethical Leadership

In Chapter 1, I noted that since the passage of the Civil Rights Act in 1964, it the prevailing legal discourse has been to prevent schools from discriminating against racial-ethnic minority students. Furthermore, I argued that based on student interviews and reports of widespread educational inequality, following the letter of the law is *not equivalent* to following its spirit. As I have also shown, the legislative tide has turned. Racial-ethnic minorities are prevalent in many public schools today; and political elites (Supreme Court justices, state attorneys-general) are manipulating legal discourse seemingly to justify discriminatory practices. In fact, emerging legal discourse threatens to make discrimination against the poor and minority working-class families "legal."

To counter the rollback of affirmative action and other admittedly imperfect strategies, school leaders must engage in what scholars of corporate culture refer to as "organizational learning." Educators must learn to resolve ethical dilemmas based on higher moral principles rather than just abiding by the letter of the law. They need to be concerned with the spirit of the law as well (Mirón & Keller, in press).

This "organizational adaptation," based on philosophical principles adopted by successful corporations, including the Ford Motor Company,[7] is in part based upon Lawrence Kohlberg's later work on the stages of moral development. I want to synthesize the scholarship on moral development by incorporating the varying perspectives of Carol Gilligan (1982) and those of Kohlberg and other critical-pragmatic scholars of educational leadership (Maxcy, 1995a; Starratt, 1994).

My ultimate goal in presenting this overview is to instill the motivation to change practice. By initiating an ethical philosophy of school leadership, examining the empirical research about organizational learning, and adopting a set of core principles to guide policy making and classroom practice in the schools, I hope that you will develop practices based on a set of *internal criteria*, the ultimate success of which only you and your school and local communities can judge.

The Appeal of Organizational Learning

At the outset, let me introduce a note of caution. Many of the concepts and practical strategies of "organizational learning" borrowed from progressive corporations may unavoidably upset my liberal colleagues. However, if I seem to have come full circle in my thinking (see Mirón, 1992), it is because I have concluded that the most noticeable impediment to progressive practices that would eradicate discrimination in schools stems from an antiquated organizational structure that allows unequal relations of power. Thus educational strategies that further the transformation of organizations, such as the ones discussed below, are drastically needed. Principals and teachers need "permission" to follow ethical standards other than those *exclusively* rooted in *external* criteria such as the law and their own districts' educational policies. By incorporating strategies from corporations engaged in organizational learning and transformation, and by embracing the overarching process values of collaboration (teamwork), we help develop moral and educational antidotes to immunize us against new forms of organizational disease.

Nurturing Stages of Moral Development

I have suggested that the "health" of schools is inexorably linked to the quality of life in the local community. This principle represents my own criteria for weighing ethical dilemmas. In organizational terms, schools reach an advanced stage of moral-ethical development when decisions that principals, teachers, and students jointly make add to the quality of life for residents in surrounding neighbor-hoods. By no means is this the only internal criterion available. Let me develop others by borrowing from scholarship that examines the organizational structures of corporations.

Sridhar & Camburn's (1993) interpretation of the work of Kohlberg (1969, 1978, 1981) suggests that the process value of com-munication (see Chapter 2) is paramount in fostering conditions that promote learning for the organization. For example, these authors do not shun conflict.

Kohlberg (1978) suggested that an individual's stage of intellec-tual development and social and educational climate would facili-tate or debilitate one's moral development. In organizational con-text, a social climate characterized by freedom of thought and communication that encourages discussion and tolerates dissent is expected to create a climate where moral reasoning is facilitated (Sridhar & Camburn, 1993, p. 730).

Two additional characteristics of the learning organization most applicable to schools are *freedom of expression* and *tolerance of ambigu-ity*. Clearly, we cannot rid public schools of identity discrimination if students feel inhibited and constrained about voicing beliefs and feelings. A climate of "emotional intelligence" needs to be cultivated. Moreover, it is difficult to imagine how we might overcome aca-demic discrimination if students, as well as parents, are locked out of curriculum policy and other decisions concerning instruction. We must seek to adopt the practices at La Escuela Fuenta (see Chapter 5) and include students in matters of governance. Furthermore, schools as learning organizations bent on achieving high levels of moral de-velopment must be capable of fostering communication that leads to a mutual respect of differences among the students themselves.

Kohlberg (1969) identified three broad categories of moral devel-opment. These are the preconventional level, the conventional level, and the postconventional level. Significantly, as organizations—con-ceptualized "as symbol processing, culture producing, and sharing entities" (see Boulding, 1956, cited in Sridhar & Camburn, 1993, p. 736)—advance through the "stages" of moral development, or-ganizational actors (teachers, principals, and students) assume pro-gressively greater, and more complex, collective roles.

The preconventional stage. At the preconventional level, moral rea-soning is guided by a simple calculus of rewards and punishments.

The preconventional stage. At the preconventional level, moral reasoning is guided by a simple calculus of rewards and punishments. According to Sridhar and Camburn, "What is 'right' or 'wrong' is judged by individuals with a concern for minimizing *personal losses* (punishment and obedience) orientation and maximizing gains (instrumental) orientation. This corresponds to Kelman's (1958) compliance orientation" (1993, p. 729, emphasis added). Simply understood, organizations at this level are isolated conglomerates of individuals acting autonomously. They are in the infancy stage of development, both morally and socially.

The conventional stage. At the next level, the conventional, the individual agent begins to change its orientation outward to the family or social group. The actors evaluate ethical dilemmas as to whether or not their resolution is socially acceptable. The organization develops a notion of morality that moves from meeting the approval of important social groups (families, colleagues) to meeting objective external criteria such as the law and preservation of the social order. I believe that the majority of public schools exhibit manifestations somewhere between the preconventional and the conventional level of moral development because law and the policies of the school officials govern most decisions affecting the school. As Henry Levin (1988) has asserted, school leaders have historically acted in their roles as policy compliers and implementers.

The postconventional stage. Finally, the most advanced or sophisticated level is the postconventional. Here the actors in the organization begin to look outside, considering the needs of society at large and the embodiment of universal principles. Although the direction is "outward," the criteria for assessing options to resolve ethical dilemmas and moral crises rest inward.

> Ethical reasoning is predicated on recognizing of moral duty to the larger society beyond one's own. Individuals define "right" and "wrong" by *self-chosen principles which often transcend those of conventional authorities*. While individuals in Stage V recognize the relativistic nature of values and norms, they are willing to reach consensus through democratic discussion and due process.[8] Individuals in Stage VI choose carefully those ethical principles which are logically comprehensive, universal and inter-

The authors note Kohlberg's admonition that rarely do individuals, much less social organizations, achieve the final stage within the postconventional level. It is extremely difficult for public schools—constructed as social organizations—to achieve high levels of ethical-moral conduct. Multiple factors account for this prognosis, not the least of which is the fact that historically, schools have developed within the context of professional cultures, which have tended to isolate the professionals who "live" inside the organization from their environment (Peterson, 1981).

Toward Moral Politics

Causes of Arrested Moral Development

Why do schools, and the system of public education that engulfs them, seem to suffer from low levels of moral development? I assert that in general, the public education system is overly standardized. Let me explain what I mean.

Most citizens naively believe that the federalist structure of governance, wherein the 50 states are legally regarded as "separate and sovereign governments,"[9] undermines a national system of public education. It does not. As historian David Tyack (1974, 1995) and others have consistently established, schools are remarkably similar in organization, curriculum, and governance. Particularly in the large metropolitan school districts, including New York, Los Angeles, and Chicago, corporate and education elites have been largely successful in constructing the "one best" system of public education.

Thus, whether legally sanctioned or not in the U.S. Constitution and the federalist structure of government, a national system of education exists. By failing to recognize the standardized nature of teaching and learning at the level of classroom activity, the public at large has been duped into believing that it has "local control" over public schools. Paradoxically, in the conduct of day-to-day instruction, classroom teachers have no power to alter this system. Nevertheless, they are able to function virtually autonomously behind the shut doors of their classrooms. Principals, too, despite the calls for instructional leadership, seem to have even less power to affect teaching and learning that moves away from standardization and toward experimentation and improvisation (Mirón, 1996; Tyack, 1974).

What educators face, then, is a no-win situation. We are caught between a rock and a hard place. The "rock" is the largely abstract system of educational governance that results in national standardization of teaching and learning. The "hard place" is the naive belief in local control that results from the dominant ideology of federalism. As former Secretary of Education Diane Ravitch put it, "if the Education Summit is a success, what we'll end up with is national standards, even if we don't want to call them that."[10] As a nation, and as a profession, we seem to want both local control and standardization.

The effect of this institutional paradox on the levels of moral development is complex. Put simply for the sake of argument, school leaders find it extremely difficult to exercise sophisticated levels of moral judgment based on *internal criteria* because *external* laws and district policies constrain them. Furthermore, the practices of professional autonomy at the school site undermine the higher possibilities for moral development at Kohlberg's postconventional level. Here, school leaders would be free to "choose carefully those ethical principles which are logically comprehensive, universal and internally consistent" (Sridhar & Camburn, 1993, p. 730). My concern with eliminating institutional racism and discriminatory practices from public schools is challenged by this moral-political dilemma. How is it possible to gain consensus for racial equality and equity as universal principles in the context of standardized classroom and school practices that reproduce discrimination? In the final section, I modestly propose a way out of this dilemma.

Modeling Moral-Ethical Standards

We need to begin with what I call a "moral politics." This means that schools, whether located in large metropolitan districts or tiny suburban enclaves, need to reaffirm *institutional* commitment to the principles of racial equality, equity, and now, social justice *at the level of daily practice*. Concretely, this means that students' personal accounts of discriminatory practices (both *identity* and *academic* discrimination) need to be taken very seriously by all of us. Students need to have voice and respect from teachers, principals, and school board members. If they say that teachers have higher expectations for white middle-class students, we need to act on this perception of inequality and unfairness.

In order to act on moral-ethical values, all educators can afford to borrow and adapt some of the restructuring models used by corporations, which have had to change their modi operandi in these times of global economic crisis and pervasive societal distrust regarding the corporate lack of concern about issues of the environment, health, and the safety of citizens. One restructuring principle has focused on placing the client first. Another, widely practiced in the Ford Motor Company under the executive leadership of Donald Peterson, is that no single person should be in charge of the organization all of the time (Levin, 1996). The emphasis is on collaborative design and organizational teamwork. In the school context, this means that students must be a part of the instructional team. To exclude them by placing excessive autonomy in the hands of principals and teachers is to undermine their needs. This change in the politics of school life will not come easily.

I am not suggesting that we turn back the progress made on the professional empowerment of teachers and improving the professional climate of public education. Teachers, of course, need respect and voice, too. In Chapter 4, I laid out strategies for a powerful means of empowerment—teacher research and inquiry. Now I want to complete the empowerment model. Empower students by taking their claims of unfair treatment in schools and classrooms seriously enough to include their perspective in governance and restructuring proposals. The political battle for racial equality and equity at the level of practice begins with student voice and school structures that empower students to feel they have some control over instruction.

Having launched the school leadership process to eliminate discrimination as a moral, universal, common good by empowering students, the next step involves meeting teachers' developmental needs. Perpetually caught between the inconsistencies of the federalist system and the dominant ideology of local control, classroom teacher-leaders need help in developing internal criteria to fulfill the universal goals of equality in their classrooms. They need an ethics of personal and societal responsibility. How do we provide that?

Let me again borrow from Sridhar and Camburn's (1993) research on ethics in corporations. By adopting these six stages of moral-ethical development within international corporations, I suggest a path to organizational learning that teachers can pursue daily. The six stages are[11] as follows:

Avoid personal harm. I find myself constantly struggling between idealism and a critical theory. In short, I am in the midst of resolving those creative tensions that mark the boundaries between vision and current reality. This stage recognizes the needs of teachers nationwide to make schools safe. Chapter 7 describes the benefits of linking up with local government, specifically with the mayor, to help schools meet community needs. Here, we move in the other direction. Let local governments assist *teachers* in making schools safe from violent crime.

Gain psychic benefits. Dan Lortie (1975) wrote about the major reason we enter the teaching profession, to make a difference in the lives of students.[12] He characterized such motivations as "psychic," as distinct from financial needs. Teachers deserve to be given the professional tools to recharge their worn-out psychic batteries. By engaging in professional development strategies such as teacher research and release time, both to attend to school restructuring and for personal growth (for example, the Unlearning Racism Seminar put on by Stir-Fry Productions in Oakland, California), teachers can recover from professional burnout.

Integrate high personal and professional norms and practices. Teachers would like to empower themselves to be able to act powerfully in their profession. In this regard, forming alliances with parents, community members, sympathetic politicians, and corporate leaders is indispensable. The idea of conforming to the norms of the profession must mean the same thing it means in other established occupations, such as the law and medicine. Though not without controversy, these professionals "police themselves" by setting their own standards of professional practice and code of ethics. Where is the code of ethics for the teaching profession?

Participate in the debate on federal, state, and local laws and district policies. In order to make moral-ethical judgments that are fair and reasonable to classroom teachers, we need to make our voices heard in state legislatures and in the halls of Congress. We also need to be more confident and clear about our own values so that students can gauge for themselves the "moral compass" in our classes. By incorporating the strategies of student governance and other forms of empowerment and voice, teachers can pass through the developmental stages leading to a classroom climate where "the thought processes occurring in later stages of moral development employ intellectual tools developed in preceding stages (facilitated by) freedom of thought and communication that encourages discussion and tolerates dissent" (Sridhar & Camburn, 1993, p. 730).

Recognize obligations to the broader school community and surrounding neighborhoods. Adopting the strategies of "team building" (see Hopfenberg, Levin, & Chase, 1993) and the process values of collaboration, communication, and community (see Chapter 2), teachers can learn to step out of their professional enclaves and alleviate isolation. Working with the entire school community (students, parents, and neighborhood leaders), classroom teachers can engage in systemic reform that enables more sophisticated levels of moral reasoning, moral leadership (Mirón & Elliott, 1994), and professional judgment. We, too, can engage in moral politics. Extending outward, we can in turn help improve the quality of life in our local communities.

Affirm the universal principle of equality for all groups of students. Admittedly the most difficult level to achieve, this stage involves twin strategies. It builds on the need to attend to the fact of unequal power relations while simultaneously recognizing interpersonal relationships in the classroom, to acknowledge both hierarchy (power) and caring (people) (Gilligan, 1982). To realize empowerment, classroom teachers must, paradoxically, relinquish some control. They can accomplish this by moving into what Argyris (1990, cited in Sridhar & Camburn, 1993, p. 731) refers to as "double loop learning." By reexamining their governing values, norms, and world views, teachers can together discover a way to enact their espoused theories of equality and equity, making these values a lived cultural reality in their classrooms. This practice will, effectively, "deconstruct" the now-abstract system of public education that encourages the keeping of power in the hands of those farthest removed from teaching. At the same time, teachers should engage in reflection and dialogue with students in order to accept personal and social responsibility for unintended discriminatory practices that harm students. They will learn to listen more fully to their students. Accepting personal responsibility for actions that have unintended negative consequences is a powerful step toward eradicating at the global level societal discrimination and institutional racism due to unequal power relations.

We Are Not the Enemy

In this book, I have sought to take a very complex phenomenon, discriminatory practice in public schools, and illustrate concrete, practical strategies for its eradication. Admittedly, this has not been an easy task. However, by laying out fully the landscape of the leadership strategies and processes that principals and teachers can take, I believe I have set a direction for the long view. By beginning the meaningful day-to-day practice of equity and social justice within the education profession, we can lay the groundwork for racial equality in all of society. For only when this country can powerfully say that, collectively, its citizens have made the practice of institutional racism morally repugnant, and therefore inconceivable, will we realize the hopes and dreams laid down by our founding mothers and fathers.

I have learned during the course of writing this book that the newspaper cartoon character Pogo was wrong: When we look inside we discover the enemy is not us! "Us" refers to educators, both professional and otherwise. In addition, the effort to reduce freedom and equality is not a national conspiracy. True, the "conservative restoration" is well under way, particularly as evidenced by the seizure of the U.S. Supreme Court, Congress, and many state capitals and local school boards. But it is far from a "done deal." The struggle for control is ongoing.

The better question is substantive and structural. *What* is the enemy? It is a dysfunctional system, which, following Velasquez (1983, cited in Sridhar & Camburn, 1993, p. 728), is poorly conceptualized as "an artificial being, invisible, intangible and existing only in contemplation of law."

Overly responsive to a system that structures moral principles according to law and district policies, educators and other civic citizens generally feel they are at risk in taking a moral stance (see Rodriguez & Gonzalez, 1996). Perhaps of even more concern is the tendency to ignore "more potent and informative causal forces such as organizational structures and decision processes which may have a bearing on unethical behavior of organizations" (Sridhar & Camburn, 1993, p. 728) such as public schools. The good news is that there are literally hundreds of examples across the country where school leaders—principals and teachers—have engaged in double-loop learning to unlearn discriminatory behaviors.

The constitutive features of the present system of public education are its tendencies toward standardization and a political-cultural context that furthers the prevailing mythology of local control and teacher autonomy. These features are diametrically incompatible. We cannot have it both ways. They combine to further professional and school cultures that leave unattended the historically unresolved moral dilemmas of democracy—discrimination and institutional racism. If this situation is not corrected, ultimately as a society we will all be victimized by the ensuing culture of schooling that enables us to ignore the resulting inequalities. By carefully implementing the strategies outlined in this book, and building from the hundreds of inspirational narratives from the field, we can, I hope, change the system. Otherwise, Pogo is correct. And in that case we will have no choice but to hold ourselves—rather than an abstract system—accountable for the suffering of our students.

Notes

1. The two articles appeared on March 17 and March 22, respectively. See Diane Seo, "Differing Schools of Thought," *Los Angeles Times,* March 17, 1996, pp. A1, A16-17; and Marc Lacey, "House OKs Bill to Curb Illegal Immigration," *Los Angeles Times,* March 22, 1996, pp. A1, A16.

2. Lynn Beck, a scholar of ethics in educational administration, who eloquently writes of "care" as a perspective by which to weigh ethical dilemmas, has recently begun conceptual work on the virtue of "forgiveness" as a philosophical problem in educational practice. Beck lectured on forgiveness to a class in school administration at the University of California, Irvine, on March 7, 1996.

3. See *Los Angeles Times,* March 26, 1996.

4. Martha Jimenez, regional counsel for the Mexican American Legal Defense Fund (MALDEF). Quoted in Amy Pyle & Patrick McDonnell, "Prop. 187 Issue Moves Onto National Stage." *Los Angeles Times,* March 22, 1996, p. A25.

5. By "conservative" I mean political, rather than philosophical or even economic, conservatism. For example, a member of the board of trustees in Garden Grove, California, complained that school leaders who sought external, and in part private, funding, to support social services were acting out of "socialist," or at least "liberal," values.

6. A very recent illustration is the ruling by the U.S. Court of Appeals on the admissions policies at the University of Texas Law School. The court panel found that: "With the best of intentions, *in order to increase the enrollment of certain favored classes of minority students,* the University of Texas School of Law . . . discriminates in favor of these applicants by giving substantial racial preferences in its admissions program. The beneficiaries of this system are blacks and Mexican Americans, to the detriment of whites and non-preferred minorities. The question we decide today . . . is whether the Fourteenth Amendment permits the school to discriminate in this way.

We hold that it does not." Appeals from the United States District Court for the Western District of Texas. Quoted in *The Chronicle of Higher Education,* Volume XLII, No. 29, p. A1, March 29, 1996 (emphasis added).

7. At a time of crisis, the CEO of Ford Motor Company, Donald Peterson, introduced a shared culture based on values of teamwork, sensitivity to customer needs, and overall quality. The underlying process value is collaboration, a principle I outlined in Chapter 7.

8. Kohlberg postulated six discrete stages within each of the three broad levels of moral development.

9. In a recent and far-reaching ruling, the U.S. Supreme Court declared it a violation of the Constitution for states to be sued for failure to comply with the laws of the federal government. See Linda Greenhouse, "Justices Curb Federal Power to Subject States to Lawsuits," *New York Times,* March 28, 1996, p. A1.

10. Ravitch was referring to the 2-day Education Summit held in Palisades, New York, on March 26 and 27, 1996. The overriding purpose of this meeting of the nation's governors and executive officers of major corporations was to devise a strategy to allow states to raise education standards and arrive at a way to measure progress.

11. I have modified the stages to conform to classroom practice. For a description of stages within the corporation, see B. S. Sridhar & A. Camburn (1993), "Stages of Moral Development of Corporations," *Journal of Business Ethics, 12,* p. 734.

12. Dan Lortie is best known for his research about social interactions as they relate to the classroom teacher.

References

Adler, L. (1996, May). *A proactive role for educators in local economic development: Shaping the future.* Paper presented to the Leadership Seminar, California State University, Fullerton.

Allen, J. E. (1995, October 4). Study: Gang killings epidemic. *Orange County Register,* p. A13.

Anderson, G., Herr, K., & Nihlen, A. (1994). *Studying your own school: An educator's guide to qualitative practitioner research.* Thousand Oaks, CA: Corwin.

Anfara, V. (1995). *The ritual and liminal dimension of student resistance to the formal culture of schooling.* Unpublished doctoral dissertation, University of New Orleans, Louisiana.

Anfara, V., & Mirón, L. F. (1996). Beyond caring: A look at practical intersubjectivity as a new paradigm for educational reform. *Journal for a Just and Caring Education, 2*(3), 304-331.

Anyon, J. (1980). Social class and the hidden curriculum. *Journal of Education, 162*(1), 67-91.

Anyon, J. (1994). The retreat of Marxism and socialist feminism: Postmodern and poststructural theories in education. *Curriculum Inquiry, 24*(2), 1-105.

Apple, M. (1985). *Education and power* (2nd ed.). Boston: ARK.

Apple, M. (1988). *Teacher and texts: A political economy of class and gender relations in education.* New York: Routledge.

Apple, M. (1993). *Official knowledge: Democratic education in a conservative age.* New York: Routledge.

Apple, M., & Beane, J. (Eds.). (1995). *Democratic schools.* Alexandria, VA: Association of Supervision and Curriculum Development.

Argyris, C. (1990). *Overcoming organizational defenses.* Boston: Allyn & Bacon.

Arias, B. M. (1986). The context of education for Hispanic students: An overview. *American Journal of Education, 96*(2), 26-57.

Ball, S. (1987). *The micropolitics of the school: Towards a theory of school organization.* London: Methuen.

Banks, J. A. (1988). *Multiethnic education: Theory and practice.* Boston: Allyn & Bacon.

Beck, L., & Foster, W. (in press). What's missing from the discourse on community? In J. Murphy and K. S. Louis (Eds.), *Handbook of research on educational administration.* San Francisco, CA: Jossey-Bass.

Beck, L. G. (1994). *Reclaiming educational administration as a caring profession.* New York: Teachers College Press.

Beyer, L., & Liston, D. (1992). Discourse or moral action: A critique of postmodernism. *Educational Theory, 42,* 371-393.

Biesta, G. (1994). Education as practical intersubjectivity: Towards a critical-pragmatic understanding of education. *Educational Theory, 44*(3), 299-313.

Bissell, J., Charlton, S., & Mirón, L. F. (1996). *ED 160: Practicum in after-school learning and inquiry.* Unpublished course proposal. Irvine: University of California.

Blase, J. (1991). *The politics of life in schools: Power, conflict, and cooperation.* Newbury Park, CA: Sage.

Bogotch, I., Mirón, L. F., & Garvin, J. (1993). Meeting national goals through community involvement: A case study. *Louisiana Educational Research Journal, 19*(1), 63-69.

Bolman, L., & Deal, T. (1991). *Reframing organizations: Artistry, choice, and leadership.* San Francisco: Jossey-Bass.

Bondi, L. (1993). Locating identity politics. In M. Keith & S. Pile (Eds.), *Place and the politics of identity* (pp. 309-330). New York: Routledge.

Boulding, K. (1956). General systems theory: The skeleton of science. *Management Science, 2*(3), 197-207.

Bourgeois, R. (1995). *In search of respect: Selling crack in el barrio.* New York: Cambridge University Press.

Bradley, A. (1995a, July 19). Daley names team in takeover of Chicago schools. *Education Week, p. 3.*

Bradley, A. (1995b, September 6). Survey of Chicago teachers paints uneven portrait of reform. *Education Week,* p. 10.

Brooks, G., & Brooks, M. G. (1993). *In search of understanding: The case for constructivist classrooms.* Alexandria, VA: Association for Supervision and Curriculum Development.

Bruesch, R. (1995, September 9). We have teachers who haven't bought into the community. *Los Angeles Times,* p. B15.

California Department of Education. (1992). *It's elementary.* (1992). Sacramento, CA: Author.

Cherryholmes, C. (1988). *Power and criticism: Poststructural investigation in education.* New York: Teachers College Press.

Chicago School Reform Act, Illinois Public Act 85-1418 (1988).

Chiu, G., Tron, T., & Chou, D. (1995). *Beyond whiz kids: The illusions behind Asian stereotypes.* University of California, Irvine: Summer Bilingual Crosscultural Language and Academic Development Institute.

City of New Orleans. (1994, June 15). *Draft empowerment plan.* New Orleans, LA: Department of Policy and Planning.

City of New Orleans. (1995, March 16). *Home rule charter of the city of New Orleans: Mayor's recommendations amendments to the charter, Ordinance Calendar No 19,882.*

Cole, M., & Olt, A. (1994, April 15). *A contested ground: Writing outside school.* Paper presented at the annual meeting of the American Educational Research Association, New Orleans, Louisiana.

Comer, J. (1980). *School Power: Implications for an intervention project.* New York: Falmer.

Community United for Fullerton Safety. (1996, March 13). *Minutes.* Orange County (California) Department of Education.

Cortés, C. (1995, May). *Education in a multicultural society. Restructuring brief.* Unpublished manuscript, University of California, Riverside.

Cowlishaw, M. L. (1995, September). *Education reform in Illinois: State and local reaction.* Illinois Association of School Boards (IASB). Alliance Legislative Alert (18-33). [On-line]. Available:

http://www.accessil.com/iasb/files/alr89-33.htm

Cremin, L. A. (1962). *The transformation of the school: Progressivism in American education, 1876–1957.* New York: Alfred Knopf.

Cummins, J. (1993). Empowering minority students: A framework for intervention. In L. Weis & M. Fine (Eds.), *Beyond silent voices:*

Class, race, and gender in United States schools (pp. 101-119). Buffalo: State University of New York.

Daly, R. (1995, June). Press conference to name new school board. *The Chicago Tribune* [On-line]. Available:

http://www.chicago.tribune.com/help/siteindx.htm

Dell, G. (1995). *A portrait of transforming teaching and learning through integrated arts.* Unpublished doctoral dissertation, University of New Orleans, Louisiana.

Devore, D., & Logsdon, J. (1991). *Crescent City schools: Public education in New Orleans, 1941-1991.* Lafayette: University of Southwestern Louisiana, Center for Louisiana Studies.

Dewey, J. (1938). *Experience and education.* New York: Macmillan.

Everhart, R. (1983). *Reading, writing and resistance.* New York: Routledge.

Epstein, J. L. (1993). A response to [Ap]parent involvement. *Teachers College Record, 94*(4), 710-717.

Fine, M. (1991). *Framing dropouts: Notes on the politics of an urban public high school.* Albany: State University of New York Press.

Fine, M. (1994). *Chartering urban school reform: Reflections on public high schools in the midst of change.* New York: Teachers College Press.

Finnan, C., St. John, E., McCarthy, J., & Slovacek, S. P. (Eds.). (1996). *Accelerated schools in action: Lessons from the field.* Thousand Oaks, CA: Corwin.

Foster, W. (1986). *Paradigms and promises: New approaches to educational administration.* Buffalo, NY: Prometheus.

Frederickson, J. (Ed.). (1995). *Reclaiming our voices: Bilingual education, critical pedagogy and praxis.* Ontario, CA: California Association of Bilingual Education (CABE).

Freire, P. (1990). *Pedagogy of the oppressed.* New York: Continuum.

Fukuyama, F. (1995). *Trust: The social virtues and the creation of prosperity.* New York: Free Press.

Garcia, E. (1994). *Understanding and meeting the challenge of student cultural diversity.* Boston: Houghton Mifflin.

Garvin, J. (1994). *Public housing and social isolation in New Orleans: A case study.* Unpublished doctoral dissertation, University of New Orleans, Louisiana.

Garvin, J., & Young, A. (1994). The politics of linking schools and social services. In L. Adler & S. Gardner (Eds.), *Resource issues: A case study from New Orleans* (pp. 93-106). Washington, DC: Falmer.

Giddens, A. (1986). *The constitution of society: Outline of the theory of structuration.* Berkeley: University of California Press.

Giddens, A. (1991). *Modernity and self-identity: Self and society in the late modern age.* Stanford, CA: Stanford University Press.

Gilligan, C. (1982). *In a different voice: Psychological theory and women's development.* Cambridge, MA: Harvard University Press.

Giroux, H. (1991). *Postmodernism, feminism, and cultural politics: Redrawing educational boundaries.* Albany: State University of New York Press.

Glickman, C. D. (1985). *Supervision of instruction: A developmental approach.* Boston: Allyn & Bacon.

Glickman, C. D. (1993). *Renewing America's schools: A guide for school-based action.* San Francisco: Jossey-Bass.

Greenhouse, L. (1996, March 28). Justices curb federal power to subject states to lawsuits. *New York Times*, p. A1.

Gullingsrud, A. (1995, August 30). *Extracurricular activities and self-esteem of Latino adolescents.* Unpublished manuscript, University of California, Irvine.

Habermas, J. (1970). Toward a theory of communicative competence. *Inquiry, 13,* 205-218.

Haymes, S. N. (1995). *Race, culture, and the city.* Albany: State University of New York Press.

Heath, S. B., & McLaughlin, M. (1993). *Inner-city youth: Beyond ethnicity and gender.* New York: Teachers College Press.

Hess, G. A., Jr. (1995, November). Chicago's new perspective on district management. *Education Week, 28,* 22.

Hopfenberg, W., Levin, H., & Chase, C. (1993). *The accelerated schools resource guide.* San Francisco: Jossey-Bass.

Jackson, P., Boostrom, R., & Hansen, D. T. (1993). *The moral life of schools.* San Francisco: Jossey-Bass.

Katz, M. (Ed.). (1971). *School reform: Past and present.* Boston: Little, Brown.

Keith, M., & Pile, S. (1993). *Place and the politics of identity.* New York: Routledge.

Kelman, H. C. (1958). Compliance, identification and internalization. *Journal of Conflict Resolution, 2,* 50-60.

Kohlberg, L. (1969). Stage and sequence: The cognitive developmental approach to socialization. In D. A. Goslin (Ed.), *Handbook of socialization theory and research*, pp. 347-480. Chicago: Rand McNally.

Kohlberg, L. (1975, June). The cognitive developmental approach to moral education. *Phi Delta Kappan, 56.*

Kohlberg, L. (1981). *Essays in moral development, volume 1: The philosophy of moral development.* New York: Harper & Row.

Kohlberg, L., Levine, C., & Hewer, A. (1983). *Moral stages: A current formulation and a response to critics.* New York: Harper & Row.

Lacey, M. (1996, March 22). House OKs bill to curb illegal immigration. *Los Angeles Times*, pp. A1, A16.

Lauria, M., Mirón, L. F., & Dashner, D. (1994). *Student resistance to the entrepreneurial coalition's drive for ideological hegemony in public schooling.* Unpublished manuscript, University of New Orleans, College of Urban and Public Affairs, Louisiana.

Lee, S. (Producer/Director). (1995). *Clockers* [Film].

Lemann, N. (1991). *The promised land.* New York: Knopf.

Levin, D. P. (1996, March 10). How Ford finally found the road to Wellville. *L.A. Times Magazine*, pp. 16-38.

Levin, H. L. (1988). *Accelerated schools for at-risk students.* New Brunswick, NJ: Center for Policy Research in Education, Rutgers University.

Lewis, D., & Nakagawa, K. (1995). *Race and educational reform in the American metropolis: A study of school decentralization.* Albany: State University of New York Press.

Lortie, D. (1975). *Schoolteacher: A sociological study.* Chicago: University of Chicago Press.

Maeroff, G. (1988, May). Withered hopes, stillborn dreams: The dismal panorama of urban schools. *Phi Delta Kappan*, 633-638.

Matute-Bianchi, M. E., & Eugenia, M. (1986). Ethnic identities and patterns of school success and failure among Mexican-descent and Japanese-American students in a California high school: An ethnographic analysis. *American Journal of Education, 96*(2), 233-255.

Maxcy, S. (1991). *Educational leadership: A critical pragmatic perspective.* New York: Bergin & Garvey.

Maxcy, S. (1995a). *Democracy, chaos, and the new school order.* Thousand Oaks, CA: Corwin.

Maxcy, S. (1995b). Beyond leadership frameworks. *Educational Administration Quarterly, 31*(3), 473-483.

McLaren, P. (1993). *Schooling as a ritual performance: Towards a political economy of educational symbols and gestures.* New York: Routledge.

McLaren, P., & Leonard, P. (1993). *Paulo Freire: A critical encounter.* New York: Routledge.

Meir, D., & Schwartz, P. (1995). Central Park East Secondary School: The hard part is making it happen. In M. Apple & J. Beane (Eds.), *Democratic schools* (pp. 26-40). Alexandria, VA: Association for Supervision and Curriculum Development.

Mirón, L. F. (1988, August). *Evaluation of the metropolitan area school-business partnership committee.* Unpublished manuscript, Loyola University of the South, New Orleans, Louisiana.

Mirón, L. F. (1991, Fall). The dialectics of school leadership: Poststructural implications. *Organizational Theory Dialogue,* 1-4.

Mirón, L. F. (1992). Corporate ideology and the politics of entrepreneurism in New Orleans. *Antipode, 2*(4), 263-288.

Mirón, L. F. (1995). Pushing the boundaries of urban school reform: Linking outcomes to community development. *Journal for a Just and Caring Education, 1*(1), 98-114.

Mirón, L. F. (1996). *The social construction of urban schooling: Situating the crisis.* Cresskill, NJ: Hampton.

Mirón, L. F., & Elliott, R. (1994). Moral leadership in a poststructural era. In S. Maxcy (Ed.), *Postmodern school leadership: Meeting the crisis in educational administration* (pp. 133-140). Westport, CT: Praeger.

Mirón, L. F., & Keller, S. (in press). Honoring the spirit of racial equality in public schools. *Thrust for Educational Leadership.*

Mirón, L. F., & Lauria, M. (1995). Identity politics and student resistance to inner-city public schooling. *Youth & Society, 27*(1), 29-54.

Mirón, L. F., & St. John, E. P. (1994). *The urban context and the meaning of school reform.* Working Paper No. 21. University of New Orleans, Division of Urban Research and Public Policy, Louisiana.

Mirón, L. F., & St. John, E. P. (1996). Implementing school restructuring in the inner-city. *Resources in Education.* (ERIC Document Reproduction Service No. ED 383 802)

Mirón, L. F., & Wimpelberg, R. K. (1989). School-business partnerships and the reform of education. *Administrator's Notebook, 33*(1), 1-4.

Murry, J. (1995). *The moral dimensions of schooling in an urban context.* Unpublished doctoral dissertation, University of New Orleans, Louisiana.

Murry, J., Bogotch, I., & Mirón, L. F. (1995, November). *Multiple interpretive frames of moral leadership.* Paper presented at the annual meeting of the Mid-South Educational Research Association, Biloxi, Mississippi.

Nakagawa, K. (1995). *Conflicting models of parent involvement: Enabling or empowering parents through school reform?* Unpublished paper, University of California, Irvine.

Noddings, N. (1992). *The challenge to care in schools.* New York: Teachers College Press.

Noddings, N. (1994). *Towards an ethic of care in the schools.* New York: Teachers College Press.

Olsen, L. (1994). *The road not taken: Creating a community-specific multicultural curriculum.* Unpublished doctoral dissertation, University of New Orleans, Louisiana.

Orleans Parish School Board. (1993, November 22). *Minutes. FNOCCA/Riverfront Project Status Report No. 1.* New Orleans, LA: Author.

Osborne, D., & Gaebler, T. (1992). *Reinventing government: How the entrepreneurial spirit is transforming the public sector.* Reading, MA: Addison-Wesley.

Peterson, B. (1995). La Escuela Fratney: A journey toward democracy. In M. Apple & J. Beane (Eds.), *Democratic schools* (pp. 58-82). Alexandria, VA: Association for Supervision and Curriculum Development.

Peterson, P. (1981). *School politics, Chicago style.* Chicago: University of Chicago Press.

Plyer v. Doe, 358 U.S. 1131 (1982).

Pyle, A., & McDonnell, P. (1996, March 22). Prop. 187 issue moves onto the national stage. *Los Angeles Times,* p. A25.

Rivera, R., & Nieto, S. (1993). *The education of Latino students in Massachusetts: Issues, research, and policy implications.* Amherst: University of Massachusetts Press.

Rodriguez, R., & Gonzalez, P. (1996, March 29). Perspectives on affirmative action. An alternative: Criminalize bigotry. *Los Angeles Times,* p. B9.

Rothstein, S. (1994). *Schooling the poor: A social inquiry into the American educational experience.* Westport, CT: Bergin & Garvey.

Santa Ana Unified School District. *Pio Pico School profile.* (1995). Santa Ana, CA: Author.

Sarason, S. (1982). *The culture of the school and the problem of change* (2nd ed.). Boston: Allyn & Bacon.

Sarason, S. (1990). *The predictable failure of educational reform.* San Francisco: Jossey-Bass.

Schlechty, P. (1990). *Schools for the 21st century: Leadership imperatives for educational reform.* San Francisco: Jossey-Bass.

Schnur, D. (1995, October 17). Speak up, General, the floor is yours. *Los Angeles Times*, p. B9.

Schon, D. (1983). *The reflective practitioner: How professionals think in action.* New York: Basic Books.

Seo, D. (1996, March 17). Differing schools of thought. *Los Angeles Times*, pp. A1, A16-A17.

Sergiovanni, T. J. (1994). *Building community in schools.* San Francisco: Jossey-Bass.

Sergiovanni, T. J. (1996). *Moral leadership: Getting to the heart of school improvement.* San Francisco: Jossey-Bass.

Soja, E. W. (1990). Heterotopologies: A remembrance of other spaces in Citadel-LA. *Strategies: A Journal of Theory, Culture and Politics, 3.*

Spencer, M. (1995). *The achievement beliefs and educational aspirations of Latino fourth and fifth graders.* Unpublished paper, University of California, Irvine, Summer Crosscultural Language and Academic Development (CLAD) Institute.

Spindler, G., & Spindler, L. (1994). *Pathways to cultural awareness: Cultural therapy with teachers and students.* Thousand Oaks, CA: Corwin Press.

Spradley, J. (1979). *The ethnographic interview.* Fort Worth, TX: Holt, Rinehart, & Winston.

Spring, J. (1985). *American education: An introduction to social and political aspects* (3rd ed.). New York: Longman.

Sridhar, B. S., & Camburn, A. (1993). Stages of moral development of corporations. *Journal of Business Ethics, 12*, 727-739.

Starratt, R. (1991). Building an ethical school: A theory for practice in educational leadership. *Educational Administration Quarterly, 27*, 185-202.

Starratt, R. (1993). *The drama of leadership.* Washington, DC: Falmer.

Starratt, R. (1994). *Building an ethical school: A practical response to the moral crisis in schools.* Washington, DC: Falmer.

Tobin, J. (1995). The irony of self-expression. *American Journal of Education, 103*, 233-259.

Troyna, B., & Hatcher, R. (1991). Racist incidents in school: A framework for analysis. *Journal of Educational Policy, 6*(1), 17-31.

Trueba, H., & Delgado-Gaitan, C. (1991). *Crossing cultural borders: Education for immigrant families in America.* New York: Falmer.

Tyack, D. (1974). *The one best system.* Cambridge, MA: Harvard University Press.

Tyack, D. (1995). Schooling and social diversity: Historical reflections. In W. D. Hawley & A. W. Jackson (Eds.), *Improving race and ethnic relations in America* (pp. 3-39). San Francisco: Jossey-Bass.

U.S. Department of Education. (1994, September). *Building community partnerships for learning.* Washington, DC: United States Government Printing Office.

Velasquez, M. G. (1983). Why corporations are not morally responsible for anything that they do. *Business & Professional Ethics Journal, 2*, 1-18.

Warner, C. (1994, June 15). Morial seeks federal windfall, empowerment zone status. *Times-Picayune,* p. A1.

Weber, M. (1968). *On charisma and institution building.* Chicago: University of Chicago Press.

Weis, L., & Fine, M. (1993). *Beyond silent voices: Class, race, and gender in United States schools.* Albany: State University of New York Press.

Willis, P. (1977). *Learning to labor: How working class kids get working class jobs.* Westmead, United Kingdom: Saxson House.

Wilson, W. (1987). *The truly disadvantaged: The inner city, the underclass, and public policy.* Chicago: The University of Chicago Press.

Wimpelberg, R., Teddlie, C., & Stringfield, S. (1989). Sensitivity to context: The past and future of effective schools research. *Educational Administration Quarterly, 25*(1), 82-107.

Suggested Resources

Books and Articles

Apple, M., & Beane, J. (Eds.). (1995). *Democratic schools.* Alexandria, VA: Association of Supervision and Curriculum Development.

Apple and Bean provide four stories of democracy from the trenches. Each chapter exemplifies students' understanding and practice of democracy within the school setting.

Batey, C. S. (1996). *Parents are lifesavers: A handbook for parent involvement in schools.* Thousand Oaks, CA: Corwin.

This book contains the real, down-to-earth skills and tips needed to turn "hard-to-reach" parents into active, sharing participants in their children's education. Written by a parent who has been there.

Hopfenberg, W., Levin, H., & Chase, C. (1993). *The accelerated schools resource guide.* San Francisco: Jossey-Bass.

Empowering the educational community is easier said than done. This guide examines school governance and decision making in order to furnish the students with the most powerful and meaningful learning possible.

Maxcy, S. (1995). *Democracy, chaos, and the new school order.* Thousand Oaks, California: Corwin.

127

*The author persuasively argues that three "process values"—commu-
nity, aesthetic intelligence, and communication—help school leaders
resolve thorny practical problems such as racism and discrimination.*

Mirón, L. F. (1996). *The social construction of urban schooling: Situating
the crisis.* Cresskill, NJ: Hampton.

*Using historical analysis, this book illustrates how educational "crises"are
largely a matter of perception. The author suggests that the greatest
challenge facing urban educators today is the tolerance of ethnic-racial
identities.*

Mirón, L. F., & Lauria, M. (1995). Identity politics and student resistance to inner-city public schooling. *Youth & Society, 27*(1), 29-54.

*Why is it that within the boundaries of an urban community two public
high schools containing similar student populations are completely different? Listen to the students' voices in this article. The answer lies
with the adults that work at each school.*

National Association of Elementary School Principals. (1994). *Best
ideas from America's blue ribbon schools: What award-winning elementary and middle school principals do.* Thousand Oaks, CA: Corwin.
National Association of Elementary School Principals. (1995). *Best
ideas from America's blue ribbon schools: What award-winning elementary and middle school principals do (Vol 2).* Thousand Oaks,
CA: Corwin.

*The best schools are learning communities. The ideas in these two col-
lections come from programs that are an example to the rest of the nation. Whether your interests are in educating for citizenship, character,
or content, or in strengthening professionalism, cooperative curriculum, and parent participation, you'll find here a treasury of suggestions
to make school a more enriching place for everyone.*

Spindler, G., & Spindler, L. (1994). *Pathways to cultural awareness: Cultural therapy with teachers and students.* Thousand Oaks, CA: Corwin.

*An edited collection for teachers, student teachers, and others who work
in the increasingly diverse world of education. The premise of the book
is that, as better informed "cultural agents," teachers and students can
learn and perform with more understanding and less resistance.*

Starratt, R. (1994). *Building an ethical school: A practical response to the moral crisis in schools.* Washington, DC: Falmer.

Starratt eloquently dispels the pessimistic view that the creation of an ethical school is nearly impossible. He also provides an elaborate process for school leaders to follow in creating this model learning environment.

Sridhar, B. S., & Camburn, A. (1993). Stages of moral development of corporations. *Journal of Business Ethics, 12,* 727-739.

The authors use Kohlberg's (1983) model of "moral development" to explain the stages organizations maintain or flow through. A case could be made for public schools applying these same stages (see Chapter 8 of this book).

Van Cleave, M. (1994) *The least of these: Stories of schoolchildren.* Thousand Oaks, CA: Corwin.

A classic story of the trials and triumphs of an elementary school principal in a poor urban neighborhood. The overriding theme is that the "human factor"—students, teachers, and principals—must be a solid part of our educational system, so that every child can receive a world-class education.

Waxman, H. C., Walker de Felix, J., Anderson, J. E., & Baptiste, H. P. (1992). *Students at risk in at-risk schools: Improving environments for learning.* Newbury Park, CA: Corwin.

A valuable practical resource for educators and students interested in at-risk, minority, and multicultural issues.

Videos

Color of Fear. Stir-Fry Productions. Oakland, CA.

A video that highlights the group dialogue methods that the "unending racism" seminars employ to heighten our awareness of stereotypes and prejudice. Although the video is aimed at adults, younger students can benefit by watching a film that explores the complex dynamics occurring when people of various races and ethnic groups interact over a series of intensive sessions.

Faces of the Enemy. Quest Productions. 2600 Tenth St., Berkeley, CA 94710.

> *This 1-hour video vividly portrays the images and metaphors that po-litical leaders throughout the globe use to depict the "enemy" (e.g., communism and the Jewish culture). The narrator makes a crucial point for classroom teachers that prior to the existence of real human enemies, or societies, there exists the idea (or image) of those individu-als or groups who threaten us. These are the stereotypes of enemies. Educators at all levels could apply these fundamental tenets to their own schools as they examine how contemporary images of enemies like criminals, gang members, and illegal immigrants become internalized as real people who threaten order in the classroom.*

Status Treatments for the Classroom. Elizabeth G. Cohen. Produced by the Program for Complex Instruction, School of Education, Stan-ford University, CA. 1994.

> *A video accompanying Cohen's book,* Designing group work: Strate-gies for the heterogeneous classroom, *2nd edition. The video pro-vides models of how to address problems of unequal status in the class-room. By working together in teams, teachers can observe each other to find out "how frequently they actually use status treatments."*

Victor. Barr Films. 12801 Schabarum Ave, Irwindale, CA, (818) 338-7878.

> *A compassionate look at the struggles of a young Mexican immigrant to find his way in American society. Torn between contradictory worlds, his home and his school, Victor often feels lost and at a loss to belong.*

Movies

Clockers. Directed by African American filmmaker Spike Lee.

> *This film reveals the consequences of identity discrimination on inner-city youth. The depiction of white police officers treating all African American youth as dangerous criminals is a powerful drama for edu-cational leaders bent on eradicating discrimination.*

Organizations

Boys' and Girls' Club.

The Boys' and Girls' Club is a nonprofit organization specializing in cocurricular and extracurricular activities for students residing in the community. President Clinton highlighted the Boys' and Girls' Club by visiting the club adjacent to Pio Pico Elementary School in 1996.

Human Relations Councils throughout municipalities across the country.

The Human Relations Council is a nonprofit organization that works closely with junior and senior high schools to eradicate bigotry and intolerance. Professional staff members from the HRC assist students, parents, and school staff in understanding and resolving issues regarding pertinent issues of human relations for educators—conflict resolution, racism, and hate crimes.

Other Resources

A World of Difference. Diversity training and curriculum. Sponsored by The Anti-Defamation League of B'nai B'rith.

A World of Difference is a curriculum provided to school personnel after several days of training. The curriculum highlights the importance as well as the beauty of multiculturalism.

Museum of Tolerance. 9786 West Pico Boulevard, Los Angeles, CA, (310) 553-8403.

This is an ideal field trip to a world-class museum for you and your students. Interactive activities are integrated into the museum's tour. The story of bigotry against the Jewish culture is presented in both a historical and an emotional context.

"The Human Family Learning to Live Together." Brochure published by The National Conference of Christian and Jews. 71 Fifth Ave, New York, NY 10003.

This national human relations organization, founded in 1927, "is dedicated to fighting bias, bigotry, and racism in America." The organization publishes a comprehensive brochure listing more than 70 titles of books for children and youth selected "because they portray people of different ethnic, racial, religious and cultural backgrounds in a way that affirms and celebrates the full range of diversity found in America and the world."

Index

**CORWIN
PRESS**

The Corwin Press logo—a raven striding across an open book—represents the happy union of courage and learning. We are a professional-level publisher of books and journals for K–12 educators, and we are committed to creating and providing resources that embody these qualities. Corwin's motto is "Success for All Learners."